"An important contribution to our understanding of the natural spirituality of children and the inner child in every adult. I recommend it heartily." —LUCIA CAPACCHIONE, author of *Recovery of Your Inner Child* and *The Creative Journal for Children*

"Ed Hoffman has made a genuine pioneering contribution in this neglected and vitally important arena of life experience." —GERALD EPSTEIN, M.D., author of *Waking Dream Therapy*

" 'For it is not in Heaven . . .' but in the innocent experience of all of us that God is heard. Dr. Hoffman's approach, so basic and direct, opens for us echoes buried in the Godyearnings and Godwrestlings of our youth, when we still dreamed the great aspiration for the noble life. It is a valuable volume to help us wake up to our inner myth—and it is not too late for us to own our own visions." —RABBI ZALMAN SCHACHTER-SHALOMI, author of *The Encounter*, co-author of *Sparks of Light*

Visions of Innocence

SPIRITUAL AND
INSPIRATIONAL
EXPERIENCES
OF
CHILDHOOD

Edward Hoffman

SHAMBHALA
Boston & London
1992

To Aaron Lev, whose newborn innocence
inspired me to write this book

Shambhala Publications, Inc.
Horticultural Hall
300 Massachusetts Avenue
Boston, Massachusetts 02115

Shambhala Publications, Inc.
Random Century House
20 Vauxhall Bridge Road
London SW1V 2SA

9 8 7 6 5 4 3 2 1

First Edition

Printed in the United States of America on acid-free paper

∞

Distributed in the United States by Random House, Inc., in
Canada by Random House of Canada Ltd, and in the United
Kingdom by Random UK Ltd.

Library of Congress Cataloging-in-Publication Data

Hoffman, Edward
Visions of innocence: spiritual and inspirational experiences of
childhood/Edward Hoffman.—1st ed.
p. cm.
ISBN 0–87773–606–5 (alk. paper)
1. Children—Religious life/Case studies. I. Title
BL625.5.H63 1992   92-50128
291.4′2′083—dc20   CIP

There was a time when meadow, grove, and stream,
The earth, and every common sight,
To me did seem
Apparelled in celestial light,
The glory and the freshness of a dream.

—WILLIAM WORDSWORTH

Contents

Contents

Preface

I have long been fascinated by the unexplored dimensions of childhood. For many years I have strongly felt that as children we feel and experience much more than most adults realize. My early milieu, a New York City neighborhood of mostly concrete streets and tenements, did not provide a very uplifting outlook on life. Far more important was the religious school I attended daily until nearly my teens. Its teachers aroused my sense of imagination and wonder in their vivid retellings of biblical legends. I was intrigued by Abraham, whose passionate quest for God originated in his childhood. The prophetic writings, hinting of a world beyond the everyday, especially stirred me. I can still recall pondering with friends the mysteries of space and time as we rode the afternoon school bus back to our homes.

Later, as a student at Cornell University in the late 1960s, I chose to major in psychology. It was an exciting time of new ideas about the mind, and I became interested in comparative religion and mysticism. Such unconventional subjects hardly penetrated my psychology classes, but that didn't matter. I pursued extensive reading and outside lectures on my own.

Then, as part of my undergraduate training, I began working educationally with children of differing backgrounds. Their energetic zeal and natural spontaneity were intense, but hardly unexpected. More surprising was my discovery that some—even as young as preschool age—seemed in their own way to be genuinely grappling with spiritual questions. Sometimes, I noticed, the "trigger" for their earnest thinking was a religious event, a vivid exposure to nature, or even an unusual dream.

At the University of Michigan I completed doctoral studies in child development. Through increasing involvement with young children I saw that some definitely had "higher" sensitivities for compassion, creativity, or aesthetics. Yet nowhere was this early capability recognized in my textbooks. Complementing my observations were scattered articles I found in publications on alternative education that featured children's poetry and vivid aphorisms. These, too, suggested a depth in childhood experience almost wholly overlooked by most educators and psychologists.

More than a decade passed as I taught college courses and did clinical work. Though I had written several books dealing with psychology and mysticism, I had devoted little attention to childhood from this vantage point until, suddenly, my interest was catalyzed in the late 1980s. At the time, I was writing a biography of Abraham Maslow, a brilliant American psychologist who argued that spirituality is basic to human nature. Pertaining to this notion, Maslow coined such popular phrases as "self-actualization" and "peak experiences"—the latter referring to those moments when we feel uplifted out of ordinary life into a realm of bliss. In researching Maslow's life, I discovered that he became convinced in his final years that children undergo peak experiences, but usually lack the means to relate them. After Maslow's first grandchild was born, he planned to begin research on this unprecedented topic in psychology. Unfortunately, the great psychologist's death from heart failure prevented the realization of this project.

In 1989, after the birth of our second child, I too felt uplifted in a special way and decided to follow Maslow's unfinished quest for the highest reaches of childhood experience. The task has been a most enjoyable one. During the past three years, my research has clearly demonstrated that childhood indeed harbors experiences and insights generally unrecognized in our time.

Visions of Innocence is hardly intended as definitive, but rather, as a gateway through which we can enter a forgotten world of beauty and order. Whether we are parents or educators, psychologists or clergy, or just interested in exploring something enduring, that youthful world surely must inspire us. If this book manages even slightly to allow us entry, then my expectations will have been fulfilled.

Acknowledgments

This book would not have been possible without the valuable cooperation of many people. Stephan Bodian, Dr. Gerald Epstein, Dr. Lawrence Epstein, Diane Hughes, Neal Kaunfer, Irene Javors, Dr. W. Edward Mann, Paul Palnik, and Alyce and Bob Tresenfeld contributed insightful ideas. I am indebted to Harvey Gitlin for his thorough research and to my parents and brother for their unstinting enthusiasm. The editorial assistance and judgment of Kendra Crossen and Samuel Bercholz are likewise considerably appreciated. I am especially grateful to the many people throughout the United States and abroad who shared their childhood spiritual experiences with me in conjunction with this book. In this book, I have identified them by pseudonyms.

On the home front, I wish to thank three individuals for their boundless patience and encouragement. My children Aaron and Jeremy, often playing beside me or insisting that I take a break, helped me stay balanced and cheerful. My wife, Laurel, more than any other person, gave me the emotional support to complete this project and fulfill my own expectations for it.

Visions of
Innocence

1

Centuries of Speculation

A man's present state may have come into conflict with his childhood state, or he may have violently sundered himself from his original character ... in keeping with his ambitions. He has thus become unchildlike and artificial and has lost his roots.

—C. G. JUNG

O N a nationally syndicated public television program, a middle-aged man with a trim beard and a warm Texas drawl is earnestly addressing a sizable viewing audience. With near-religious intensity, befitting his seminary training, he speaks movingly about the psychology of addiction and its roots in childhood trauma. Often referring to his own abusive upbringing and adult struggle for emotional health, this influential psychotherapist-educator—John Bradshaw—repeatedly emphasizes the lasting importance of our earliest years. Gazing into the television camera, he urges the viewer to "embrace your lost inner child."

"Sit in an upright position," Bradshaw intones. "Relax and focus your breathing." After initiating this preparatory relaxation, he gently conveys a powerfully healing guided image to millions who sit with eyes intently closed—of the small, forgotten child who is our past self yet who still lives within each of us.

In a manner hardly imaginable a decade ago, an increasing number of people across North America and abroad are recognizing that strengthening the link to our childhood self is crucial for achieving greater happiness and balance in everyday life. Undoubtedly, several factors are catalyzing this awareness. For one thing, men and women who have long suffered from early trauma are no longer as willing to hide inwardly in shame. Thanks to the work of health professionals and support-groups patterned after the "twelve steps" of Alcoholics Anonymous, even public figures are now beginning to acknowledge openly their past victimization through physical, emotional, or sexual abuse. By courageously facing the "wounded child" within, they are helping countless others to initiate a healing process that can ultimately lead to true well-being.

Yet another impetus for seeking the inner child comes from contemporary parents, especially those belonging to the immense baby-boom generation that came to maturity in the late 1960s and 1970s. Having embraced spiritual and transpersonal values in charting their life course to date, they are now seeking to raise children in accordance with these same personal ideals. Likewise, many educators nowadays are voicing their conviction that in our turbulent society we must provide youngsters with a strong moral sensibility and a deep respect for their natural environment.

In the fields of counseling and psychotherapy, mechanistic approaches to personality study and treatment are giving way to the notion that human spirituality is an important and inborn characteristic. More and more practitioners are realizing that unless we recognize our higher longings and sensitivities, the goal of self-fulfillment is likely to remain elusive. The search for the inner child and the quest for more meaningful values lead naturally to a desire to acknowledge and re-experience moments of spiritual awakening in childhood. Such moments can not only connect us to our forgotten past but also rekindle long-dormant religious impulses.

Before exploring directly the nature of childhood's most exalted moments, it may be helpful first to examine how this intriguing subject has been approached over the centuries. Though it is not intended to be exhaustive, the historical survey that follows may provide a valuable perspective to guide us.

Religious Views of Childhood

Historically, the world's great religions have always recognized our childhood capacity for closeness to the divine. The Bible tells us in Psalms that God's "glory above the heavens is chanted by the mouths of babes and infants." The prophet Isaiah predicted a future age of earthly harmony in which "the wolf shall dwell with the lamb, and the leopard shall lie down with the kid, and a little child shall lead them." Jewish mysticism has for millennia taught that during our fetal existence we are exposed to the radiant secrets of the universe, but at the moment of birth we are made to forget such knowledge in order to fulfill our purpose here on earth.

As recorded in the Gospels, Jesus, when asked by his disciples, "Who is the greatest in the kingdom of heaven?," called to a child and placed him in their midst. "Unless you turn and become like children," he declared, "you will never enter the kingdom of heaven." In another episode, Jesus defended the presence of children in a crowd gathered around him. "Do not hinder them, for to such belong the kingdom of heaven. Truly, I say to you: whoever does not receive the kingdom of God like a child shall not enter it."

The notion that childhood may harbor special intuitive and

spiritual sensitivities has long flourished in Western religion. In Kabbalistic practice during the Middle Ages, young children were sometimes asked to gaze into a polished surface, such as a crystal, a mirror, or a hand's palm smeared with soot and oil, and describe what they saw with their imagination. On the basis of the replies, mystical adepts would make predictions about the future or far-off events. This was the only accepted form of Jewish divination at the time, one that was also practiced by medieval Christians.

In Roman Catholicism children have for centuries been regarded as having a special affinity for the Virgin Mary and an ability to receive celestial visitations. During World War I in Fátima, Portugal, three children together reported such encounters involving prophetic messages about the war and historical events to come. The final encounter was accompanied by extraordinary atmospheric occurrences that were witnessed by thousands of local inhabitants. Eventually, the church heads in Rome became convinced that something truly mystical had transpired and eagerly received the secret prophecies from the children.

Currently, the controversial Catholic priest Matthew Fox has stressed what he calls "honoring the child within." In his cogent viewpoint, our society is suffering from so many disorders because we are neglecting a vital task of nurturance: "In this failure to honor our children and the child within lies one of the most critical dangers of our epoch—and ironically, one of the most powerful sources for a global renaissance."[1] Fox argues that in order to heal the wounded child inside us, it is necessary to make connection with the divine child once again.

Apart from the few examples I have given, it would be inaccurate to suggest that institutional religions in the West have consistently embraced a warm, favorable attitude toward childhood spirituality. In contrast, non-Western and shamanic cultures have generally regarded childhood as part of the inextricable web of human existence in a spiritual universe. That is, they have not tended to isolate youthful experience as something necessarily immature or nonsensical, but rather, as valid in its own right.

According to oral accounts by generations of Native American healers and shamans, tribal elders traditionally recognized a special, inner sensitivity in certain youngsters. Sometimes the presence of such a natural gift might reveal itself through the child's dream or waking vision. The elders might then initiate specific tutoring or apprenticeship to spur the child's spiritual growth.

In his provocative book *The Vision*, wilderness training expert Tom Brown writes about his spiritual mentor, "Grandfather," born into a small nomadic clan of Lipon Apaches during the 1880s. At the age of ten Grandfather experienced a powerful vision while alone in the wilderness and promptly reported it to his tribe's elders. They convened a special council, before whom the boy was told "that the vision and the spirit had guided him toward a path he must take. To follow his vision, he must first spend ten winters training to become a scout, one of the most powerful positions in the tribe. He must then abandon this path for another ten winters and seek the path of a shaman and healer. And finally, the elder named 'Coyote' told him, he would have to leave his people and wander alone for sixty more winters, seeking vision and knowledge, until his vision was reality."[2]

Nearly all tribal cultures have rites of initiation, demarking childhood's passage into another realm of earthly existence. Among many Native American tribes, such initiation usually involved a "vision quest" or "crying for a vision," in which the youth experienced an intense awakening about the spiritual purpose of his or her life. The present-day Sioux shaman

Lame Deer has recalled about his own childhood vision quest, in which he was left alone in the mountains without food or water for four days: "Of course, when it was all over, I would no longer be a boy, but a man. I would have my vision. I would be given a man's name."[3]

The Visionary Poets:
Blake and Wordsworth

The age-old initiatory traditions lasted for many centuries in the West. But the rise of the industrial age began to shatter longstanding cultural rites and patterns of spirituality. In particular, the factory system inflicted unprecedented horrors on children. Such wretched working and living conditions, vividly depicted by the English novelist Charles Dickens, were historically unprecedented. They were eventually eliminated, or at least reduced, through public outcry, leading to to parliamentary action.

Paradoxically, the same era in England witnessed the appearance of two remarkable visionary poets who, in quite different ways, venerated childhood as the most exalted period of human life: William Blake (1757–1827) and William Wordsworth (1770–1850). Perhaps more than any other identifiable figures in modern Western history, they regarded our early years as inherently wondrous and close to God. For those of us today seeking a path to the visionary "peaks" of childhood experience, Blake and Wordsworth are key guides.

William Blake was born and raised in London, the city that was to be his home through nearly his entire life. His parents were "free thinkers" who rejected conventional Christianity and embraced instead the more mystical teachings of Emanuel Swedenborg. They tutored William privately at home and, when he showed artistic talent, sent him to a teacher for art lessons in London's Strand section. Though not poor, William's parents could not afford to enroll him in art school. He was therefore apprenticed at the age of fourteen to a well-known engraver. After six years Blake embarked on a financially uneven but creatively magnificent career that blended poetry, painting, engraving, and printing.

Blake's most inspiring and important work on childhood was his illustrated book of poems *Songs of Innocence*, which Blake self-published in 1789. The author was thirty-two years old, happily married, and part of a lively group of free-spirited artists and writers who regularly met and included the feminist Mary Wollstonecraft and the revolutionist Thomas Paine. Later in life, a more embittered Blake would espouse a darker vision of ordinary human existence; but in *Songs of Innocence* he offered a radiant image of childhood as the time when our joy and innocence—and above all, our ability to live fully in the moment—are supreme.

The book opens with the famous lines:

> Piping down the valleys wild,
> Piping songs of pleasant glee,
> On a cloud I saw a child,
> And he laughing said to me:
>
> "Pipe a song about a Lamb!"
> So I piped with merry cheer.

Using the style of popular ballads and deliberately simple poetic forms, Blake not only depicted but *evoked* the magical purity of childhood perception. In our earliest years, Blake poetically suggested, we live without labeling or dividing the world into abstract categories. Thus we feel a natural kinship with all that we behold. Earth does not need to be contrasted

with heaven: it is itself heaven. Even a commonplace village
green becomes a shining and rapturous place from Blake's
understanding of childhood:

> The sun does arise
> And make happy the skies.
> The merry bells ring
> To welcome the Spring.
> The skylark and thrush
> The birds of the bush
> Sing louder around
> To the bells' cheerful sound
> While our sports shall be seen
> On the Echoing Green.

As a visit to any spring playground readily reveals, this
vision remains true even two centuries later. For Blake, childhood is unique in this way because we experience everything
under the canopy of eternity. That which has been and that
which may be have almost no place in a child's outlook—the
here-and-now is central. In a sense, the seemingly inevitable
laws of time and decay are temporarily suspended. For this
reason, felt Blake, our first years have prophetic significance.
They herald a time on earth when all humanity will regain its
childhood innocence and delight:

> In futurity
> I prophetic see
> That the earth from sleep
> (Grave the sentence deep)
>
> Shall arise and seek
> For her maker meek;
> And the desert wild
> Become a garden mild.

In portraying childhood as a spiritually dazzling period of life, Blake drew from his own experience. He had sublime visions almost as soon as he could speak, and they came to him throughout his life. When only four years old, he told his wife decades later, he saw "God's face" at the window of his room and screamed in fear. As a child Blake was beaten for relating that he had seen the prophet Ezekiel sitting in a nearby tree. On another occasion Blake beheld a tree filled with angels, who sang and waved their radiant wings in the branches.

Aside from such exotic perceptions, the young Blake appears also to have possessed the gift of character discernment. At the age of fourteen he refused to be apprenticed to a famous engraver named Ryland because the man "looked as if he would live to be hanged." Indeed he was, several years later, for criminal forgery against the king.

Blake did not view all childhood experience as inherently wonderful. He was well aware of the misery that the Industrial Revolution was bringing to London and other major cities in England. Not long after *Songs of Innocence* was published, Blake's poems became filled with references to the injustice of child industrial labor, and he gave the English language the memorable phrase "dark satanic mills" to describe these moral blights on England's fair landscape. Yet he always retained his conviction that our childhood sense of eternity and joy is an accurate perception of the world. Similarly, cynicism and despair for Blake represented grossly inappropriate and inaccurate ways of responding to the divine that dwells within all things.

Blake was a true visionary who died largely unappreciated in his own era. At the time of his death in 1827, most who had heard of Blake dismissed his work as that of a struggling eccentric. But today he is revered as a poet and artist who guided us in better seeing "a World in a Grain of Sand . . ./ And Eternity in an hour."

William Wordsworth, though quite a different visionary, likewise offered a profound conception of childhood spirituality. Wordsworth was born and raised in England's pastoral Lake District. There, as he later recalled in his great autobiographical poem *The Prelude*, the beautiful River Derwent flowed gently past his backyard, giving him "among the fretful dwellings of mankind, a knowledge . . . of the calm which Nature breathes among the hills and groves."

A year after he became orphaned at the age of thirteen, young Wordsworth began writing poetry. Like Blake he discovered his life's calling at an early age when prone to unusual episodes of introspection and silence. The first poetry that Wordsworth wrote spontaneously (that is, not for a school assignment) was written in 1784, after he had walked home late from a dance. Most of his visions—his dreamlike trances—occurred on his walks, even on the half-mile or so walk from his lodgings to school. He usually extended this stroll to a five-mile saunter by going around the lake.

"I was often unable," Wordsworth commented years later, "to think of external things as having external existence. I communicated with all I saw as something not apart from, but inherent in my own immaterial nature. Many times while going to school have I grasped at a wall or a tree to recall myself from this abyss of idealism to the reality."[4]

Wordsworth received his bachelor's degree from Cambridge in 1791. He had declared no major and declined to sit for full examinations, and therefore was graduated without honors. He loved writing poetry, and the only real value he attributed to his university education was that it convinced him to have nothing to do with the careers of law or the clergy. After floundering a bit emotionally during his early twenties,

Wordsworth struck up friendship with his fellow poet Samuel Taylor Coleridge, near whom he settled in the Lake District. By 1800 Wordsworth felt that his destiny was to live there peacefully and write poetry, and this he did for the rest of his long life.

Nearly all literary critics—and perhaps Wordsworth himself—regarded his most productive years as occurring before the age of thirty-five. Historical evidence suggests that the growing responsibilities and financial pressures of marriage and fatherhood dampened his early creativity. In any event, Wordsworth's major poetry concerned childhood and nature, and he elaborated stunningly beautiful verses on these themes. Quite deliberately, he chose the medium of poetry rather than prose to express his mystical ideas about the world.

More than any other poet in the English language, Wordsworth was enraptured with childhood experience. For him, childhood by its very nature had an ineffable splendor, imbued with a glory associated with its fresh and pure perception. In this regard, Wordsworth viewed children as oracles, capable of seeing truths that we adults can no longer discern, or have forgotten, as a result of our mundane, habit-worn lives. "The world is too much with us," he poignantly remarked, at least somewhat autobiographically, in one poem; "late and soon, / Getting and spending, we lay waste our powers."

Wordsworth's most exalted portrayal of childhood is found in his "Ode: Intimations of Immortality from Recollections of Early Childhood." In the words of one biographer, it is "the greatest of Wordsworth's poems and that to which all others lead up."[5] Another biographer calls it "the profoundest and richest expression of Wordsworth's faith in the unsullied purity of the child's intuitions."[6] In this poem Wordsworth conveys his mystic conviction that during our childhood the gates of heaven lie open all around us. We may not be able to verbalize such awareness—even as adults, we can scarcely articulate our "peak" or transcendent experiences. But Wordsworth's opening lines recall with surety:

> There was a time when meadow, grove, and stream
> The earth, and every common sight,
>   To me did seem
>   Apparelled in celestial light,
> The glory and the freshness of a dream.

Wordsworth depicts childhood as the most sacred period of our human existence, filled with a brilliant and "visionary gleam." In the ode's subsequent lines he elaborates the mystical philosophy that we have all lived in eternity before being physically born. For this reason, our earliest years are precisely those closest to divinity. The fifth stanza begins:

> Our birth is but a sleep and a forgetting;
> The Soul that rises with us, our life's Star,
>   Hath had elsewhere its setting,
>   And cometh from afar;
>   Not in entire forgetfulness,
>   And not in utter nakedness,
> But trailing clouds of glory do we come
>   From God, who is our home.

Seized by such a potent vision of human spirituality, Wordsworth insisted throughout his life on the right of every child to enjoy happiness and freedom within a loving family. Like Blake, he railed against the suffering and degradation brought by industrialization and protested the moneyed outlook that sought to justify child labor. For Wordsworth, we most fulfill our purpose on earth when we venerate childhood, both in ourselves and others.

Modern Psychology and Childhood Spirituality

The father of modern psychotherapy and personality theory, Sigmund Freud (1856–1939), was highly antagonistic toward the entire subject of spirituality. Raised in an assimilated Austrian Jewish family, Freud was a lifelong atheist who contemptuously dismissed mysticism as nothing more than an immature regression to the "oceanic experience" of the womb.

As a proud rationalist, Freud regarded childhood as a time in which our lowest, most animalistic impulses are strongest. For Freud, the infant and toddler are nearly all "id"—that is, seething with instinctual drives for self-gratification. He saw the preschool years as dominated by incestuous longings that ultimately require strict inner suppression. It is hard to imagine a picture of childhood more alien to the reverential delight of Blake and Wordsworth.

Freud's closest intellectual ally for several years, the Swiss psychiatrist Carl Gustav Jung (1875–1961), decisively broke with Freud in 1913 to forge his own systematic explanation of the human psyche. Jung, far more sympathetic to spirituality than was Freud, delved deeply into such exotic spheres as Eastern philosophy and mysticism, cross-cultural mythology, fairy tales, religious art, and alchemy. Nevertheless, Jung had little to say about the numinous experiences of childhood. In fact, he believed that we become keenly interested in visionary experience only during the second half of life.

Late in Jung's career, though, he seemed to shift his position somewhat. His autobiography, *Memories, Dreams, Reflections*, written in the late 1950s, contains significant material about his early years. After describing a strange childhood dream rich with powerful imagery and symbolism, Jung remarks:

> It was only fifty years later that a passage in the study of religious ritual burned into my eyes, concerning the motif of cannibalism that underlies the symbolism of the Mass. Only then did it become clear to me how exceedingly sophisticated was the [childhood] thought that had begun to break through into [my] consciousness. . . . Who was it speaking in me? What kind of superior intelligence was at work? . . . Who talked of problems far beyond my knowledge? Who brought the Above and Below together, and laid the foundation for everything that was to fill the second half of my life with stormiest passion? Who but that alien guest who came both from above and below?[7]

In the same intriguing work Jung also recalls how at age seven or nine, he used to sit by himself on a boulder near his pastoral home and become wrapped in philosophical wonderment:

> Often, when I was alone, I sat down on this stone, and began an imaginary game that went something like this: "I am sitting on top of this stone and it is underneath." But the stone could also say "I" and think: "I am lying here on this slope and he is sitting on top of me." The question then arose: "Am I the one who is sitting on top of the stone, or am I the stone on which *he* is sitting?" This question always perplexed me . . . and my uncertainty was accompanied by a feeling of curious and fascinating darkness.[8]

Aside from such recollections about his own experience, Jung said little about childhood spirituality. In this respect he was unfortunately typical of the whole current of mainstream psychology and its therapeutic offshoots. Even William James, who as the founder of American psychology at the turn of the twentieth century possessed a keen interest in religious experience, never really turned his attention toward the early years. This widespread lack of interest persisted for decades until, beginning in the 1960s, there arose a glimmer of professional interest in this evocative topic. Abraham Maslow (1908–70), who had helped foster the new movements of humanistic and then transpersonal psychology, became convinced that children undergo genuine "peak experiences." This was the term Maslow had coined a few years before to describe those moments in our lives when we feel most inspired, fulfilled, and exalted. Maslow conjectured that some children, perhaps from birth onward, are more disposed than others to such episodes.

More recently, interest in spirituality during the early years has emerged from two rather different spheres of psychology. The first comes from therapeutic work with children who are terminally ill or have nearly died as a result of sickness or accident. Undoubtedly, Dr. Elisabeth Kübler-Ross has been a key pioneer in this domain. As the author of many immensely popular books, including *On Death and Dying*, Dr. Kübler-Ross startled the medical and scientific world in the late 1970s by asserting that her work with the terminally ill had led her directly into the realm of transcendent experience.

"I have been criticized for 'getting involved in spiritual matters,' " Dr. Kübler-Ross has written, "since I was trained in the 'science' of medicine. I have been called every possible name ... I have been labeled, reviled, and otherwise denounced. . . . But it is impossible to ignore the thousands of stories that dying patients—children and adults—have shared with me. These illuminations cannot be explained in scientific language."[9]

Medical practitioners like Kübler-Ross and Raymond Moody have repeatedly found that terminally ill children often acquire an uncanny quality of wisdom and inner peace. Not only do they frequently seem emotionally unfettered by their physical impairment, but they are even able to offer uplifting solace to adult family members grieving over them. Many adults have reported that such children often seem "wise beyond their years," as though their life-threatening illnesses accelerated their spiritual maturation.

Perhaps even more intriguing are the findings of Dr. Kübler-Ross, Dr. Moody, and others pertaining to childhood near-death experiences (NDEs). These investigators have reviewed countless reports, some by children as young as two years, that consistently describe a common series of extraordinary events close to the moment of physical death. The NDE accounts of both adults and children typically mention passing through a tunnel, encountering a divinelike presence of light and feeling overwhelming serenity and joy, and having contact with loved ones who have already died. While scientific proof for such accounts is still lacking, they are certainly suggestive and deserve further study. As Dr. Kübler-Ross has observed, "I can only say that these [episodes] come from every corner of the world—from religious and non-religious people, believers and non-believers, from every conceivable cultural and ethnic background."[10]

As highlighted at the beginning of this chapter, interest today in childhood spirituality has also arisen through therapeutic programs for adults suffering from various addictive disorders. Programs such as those based on the "twelve steps" to inner recovery are also helping men and women who have been victimized by childhood trauma or sexual abuse, including incest. In this regard, popular authors like John Bradshaw, Alice Miller, and Charles Whitfield have emphasized that within each of us—no matter how wretched we may feel—lies an inviolate "inner child" that possesses innocence, purity, and a full capacity for joy. Though the context is quite different, their psychological message is similar to that of Blake and Wordsworth. Thus Bradshaw comments in his moving book *Healing the Shame That Binds You*: "The magical child emerges when the wounded inner child is embraced and nourished. Our true self is eternal and enduring. It persists throughout all change. It survives as our Magical Child."[11]

A New Look at Childhood Spirituality

In order to gain more knowledge about childhood spirituality, I decided to conduct empirical research. Initially, my plan was to interview children themselves. I soon found, however, that they generally lacked the ability to relate their subtle experiences meaningfully. This was hardly surprising, since even articulate adults find it difficult to communicate their peak or transcendental episodes. Children are more proficient in verbalizing their specific reactions to formalized religious activity, such as church or synagogue worship or biblical study. Similarly, youngsters can fairly readily answer questions about their moral or religious beliefs, such as "What is God?"

Other writers have at least begun to investigate these worthwhile issues. My primary goal instead was to explore spontaneous occurrences of great meaning, beauty, or inspiration during our early years—apart from institutional religion. To this end, I chose to gather reports from adults who could recall such childhood experiences.

In order to gain a sample as representative and wide-ranging as possible, I placed an author's query in dozens of newspapers and periodicals circulating throughout the English-speaking world, including the United States, Canada, Great Britain, and Australia. Some publications were broad-based in their readership, such as the *Los Angeles Times Book Review*. Others were aimed at professional counselors or psychotherapists. Still others appealed to specific religious audiences (Catholics, Jews, members of the various Protestant denominations) or those with nonsectarian interests in Eastern philosophy and comparative religion.

Within a few months an article describing my ongoing research appeared in a German magazine and generated additional responses from European readers. Their letters were translated into English and then combined with my total sample. In addition, I solicited reports from individuals with whom I was personally acquainted, often through their creative work in the arts.

Each respondent in my study was asked: "Can you recall any experiences from your childhood—before the age of fourteen—that could be called mystical or intensely spiritual? Or, to put it another way: Can you recall any childhood moments in which you seemed to experience a different kind of reality—perhaps involving a sense of rapture or great harmony? As a child, you may or may not have recognized the experience as extraordinary or unusual, but think now from your current vantage point. I am especially interested in childhood experiences or perceptions that have endured in your memory and may have permanently affected your view of life or death, God, the universe, or the nature of human existence."

All respondents were also asked to provide personal information: present age and occupation, birth order, where and at what age each experience occurred, and childhood religious affiliation, if any. The vast majority of interviews were conducted in writing. Sometimes, though, I found it necessary to perform a follow-up interview by phone in order to gain a more thorough understanding of the particular reminiscence.

Like Abraham Maslow and other researchers interested in real-life (rather than laboratory) situations, I adopted a phenomenological approach, allowing people to speak in their own words about the most memorable spiritual experiences of childhood. Certainly, as a practicing clinical psychologist I recognized that adults may not always recall with total accuracy events that happened many decades ago. Yet I hoped that a clear enough pattern might emerge to provide new information on this important topic.

Over a period of approximately eighteen months, I received over 250 written or oral accounts from men and women around the globe. Their ages ranged from the mid-eighties down to the early twenties, plus a rather articulate sixteen-year-old. Likewise, the childhood religious backgrounds of respondents were surprisingly varied. I also received a few unsolicited narratives from parents interested in sharing pertinent anecdotes about their children. (I will comment in greater detail on the sample in chapter 11.)

My next step was to select the most relevant and articulate reports and organize them systematically. Perhaps most frequently I eliminated those describing merely unusual or "paranormal" occurrences without enduring significance to the narrator. The third stage of my research, establishing a typology of experience, initially proved far more difficult than I had anticipated. Undoubtedly, this situation was due to the open-ended and highly individualistic character of the accounts. After several false starts, however, I was able to establish nine distinct (but inevitably overlapping) categories of childhood spiritual experience, which are highlighted in the next nine chapters:

· Uplifting experiences in places of scenic grandeur
· Inspiring encounters with nature in one's own backyard
· Near-death or crisis episodes
· Peak moments during intense and personalized prayer
· Spontaneous moments of bliss or ecstasy
· Profound insights about self-identity and God, life and death, and related topics
· Exalted experiences in formal religious settings
· Uncanny perceptions with lasting import
· Unforgettable dreams

Certainly, other forms of grouping are possible in future exploration of this field. For now, however, these nine categories have proven useful for their empirical validity as well as the structure they offer upon which to build interpretation and theory.

As you ponder these multifaceted and fascinating accounts, you will undoubtedly see interconnections and patterns among them. In several instances, male and female respondents from quite different backgrounds have presented amazingly similar and yet uncommonly uplifting accounts. To me, this fact emphasizes the universality of our inborn spiritual nature. While recognizing the exploratory nature of this study, I have in the final chapter offered my major conclusions and their practical implication for all seeking to honor, in the best possible way, the childhood experience still living within us.

2

The Grandeur of Nature

Each new year is a surprise to us. We find that we had virtually forgotten the note of each bird, and when we hear it again, it is remembered like a dream, reminding us of a previous state of existence. . . . The voice of nature is always encouraging.

—HENRY DAVID THOREAU

*I*T has become almost a truism to say that nature has the power to induce in us intense feelings of awe. People of all cultures and places have always experienced this grandeur in ways that exalted their lives. Undoubtedly, it was not necessary for individuals to be artists or poets in order to draw inspiration from the majestic beauty around them. In contemporary society, however, our urbanized way of life leaves us little opportunity for such uplifting moments. Aside from infrequent vacations, we seldom have exposure to nature's wide vistas. Even when we take such summer or holiday excursions, ongoing pressures often make it hard for us to really see and feel what we are seeking in the mountains, seashore, or countryside.

This aspect of modern life has been apparent for at least two centuries—so much so that, as I mentioned in chapter 1, the early Romantics often linked nature and childhood in their stirring poetic depictions. Was their vision simply the result of wishful thinking or imaginative fancy? It seems not, for the representative accounts that follow reveal youthful bliss or ecstasy experienced as a direct result of nature's splendor. Men and women from strikingly varied backgrounds and locales are thereby united in their lifelong memories of such exalted moments. By listening to these reports, we can surely begin to reestablish the lost connection to nature in our own lives.

In the Adirondack Mountains

Roslyn is a seventy-year-old retired teacher who has spent most of her life in New Jersey. An only child, she was adopted by an intellectually oriented and nonreligious couple in their forties. "Getting close to nature was important for them," Roslyn recalls, "and when I was three, my parents first took me camping for several days in the Adirondack Mountains of upstate New York. The camp was located in a small clearing at the edge of a clear lake, and our tent was quite close to the lake's edge.

"One night I awoke quietly and slipped out of the tent, past both my slumbering parents. Outside, the mountain darkness was incredibly intense. Only a pale moonlight illumined the wild landscape. For a moment I felt afraid about what might be lurking behind the towering trees surrounding our small clearing. Then I turned toward the lake and looked up at the deep, black sky filled with stars.

"It seemed as though the sky and the stars were reaching right toward me. Suddenly I had a warm and joyful sense of being absorbed into this enveloping scene. Though I certainly lacked the vocabulary at the time, I absolutely *knew* that I belonged there, and was somehow integrally connected. I was reluctant to go back to the tent, and stood gazing at the sky and the silent lake for a long, long time.

"It must have been my second summer in the Adirondacks," Roslyn recollects, "that I developed a special attachment to a certain tree at the camp. It made me feel welcome, and I regarded it as my friend. In fact, one of my earliest childhood memories is stretching my small frame along its trunk and hugging it.

"I liked the trunk's warm, rough surface. Its life and strength seemed to flow into me. The tree was one of many along the shady path to the little beach on the island. Sitting under its leafy canopy, shielded from the hot sun and away from the open campsite, I knew I had found a real place of my own. I was away from other people, where I could be myself and yet part of a strong life force *beyond* myself.

"Each year as we prepared to leave the campsite, I said good-bye to the tree. Upon returning to the camp the following year, the first thing I always did was to make sure my 'special tree' was still there.

"That tree was my place of refuge. I didn't want to tell anyone about it. I feared that something might happen to the tree if other people knew about it. Adults wouldn't understand, and my cousin was always trying to destroy or damage things that I cared about.

"But last summer," Roslyn continues, "my cousin and I returned to the Adirondack wilderness and that particular lake for the first time in sixty years. We paddled a rented canoe to the island campsite, and slowly walked up the long-familiar shaded path.

"My beloved tree was still standing there! All the same childhood feelings I had experienced returned in full force to me. Because my cousin was there, I didn't touch the tree. To do so just wouldn't have felt right. Instead, I allowed it to physically remain a sacred memory.

"I did take a photograph, however, and returned to gaze at

the tree several more times. As the two of us got ready to leave, I said a silent good-bye to it. The tree has been a profound experience for my life."

The Voice of Nature

Inga is a thirty-three-year-old woman who has spent her entire life in Germany. An only child, she grew up in a nonreligious family: "Our home was in the city, but fortunately we lived only a few minutes away from a beautiful park with many kinds of flowers. There were no other children my age in our apartment complex, and because both my parents worked, I was obliged to play alone most of the time. On Sundays we made trips regardless of the weather to the nearby Harz Mountains. There I played hiding games or had picnics.

"I can't remember if my parents ever told me that nature is alive or has a certain spirit," Inga comments. "But I always felt that nature had a definite soul. In our backyard an old maple tree stood, and I used to climb up it and spend many hours amid its branches. I would hug this old tree, and I always felt that it spoke to me. Its branches and leaves were like arms hugging and touching me, especially on windy days. Years later my mother told me how she had often worried that I would suddenly fall out and die.

"Not only the trees could speak to me, but also all the plants, streams, and even the stones. In the Harz Mountains we would often picnic next to a certain brook. In those years there were few tourists, and I'd frequently sit for hours without moving and listen to its sound. When I would find an especially beautiful rock on the road, I would take it, feel it, observe it, smell it, taste it, and then listen to its voice. Afterward, I would return happily to my parents and relate what the trees or flowers, rocks or brook had told me. They would find this amusing, and were proud of their daughter's imagination.

"It was a beautiful time," recalls Inga, "full of something that today I can't find words to describe. Even normal things like the slow movement of clouds across a windy sky, or the sound of the fire crackling in the oven, were wondrous and miraculous to me. Nature was more interesting and exciting than any fairy tale I would read at night.

"Then school began, and everything changed. Because of my intense involvement with nature, I couldn't relate well to other children, who seemed silly and babyish to me. They found me strange and funny. But even harder was the change at home. Until then, my parents had encouraged me to talk about my conversations with trees or rocks. But now they denied everything with the words: 'What nonsense! The rocks can't talk! Don't let anybody hear this, because they'll think you're crazy!'

"How right my parents were. I found out one day when my classmates saw me talking to a big chestnut tree in front of the schoolyard. Not only did they ridicule me, but they told the teacher, who requested a meeting with my parents the next day. She told them to watch their daughter even more closely, because 'Inga fantasizes too much and could easily lose her connection to reality.'

"My parents recounted the conversation to me and clearly showed how ashamed they were 'to have such a crazy child.' From that day onward, my magic was systematically ruined or destroyed. If I made any comments about animals, trees, flowers, brooks, or rocks, my parents would call it 'utter nonsense.' When that remark didn't change my feelings, they threatened to beat me.

"So it happened," Inga concludes, "that I started believing that nature was mute and couldn't speak to me. But I kept searching for something and became an avid reader, especially of fairy tales and myths. By the time I was twelve I was already writing short stories to express myself. The end of my spiritual searching came in my early twenties, when I discovered the historical existence of nature religions.

"In my circle with others, we seek to harmonize with nature as fully as possible. What does this mean? Being closely aware of the seasons and experiencing our lives as part of nature. Through my early, intensive contact with nature, it's easier for me to remember what others as adults must learn. My life is once again happy, because I've found the soul of nature."

Opening into the Ocean

Elaine is a forty-four-year-old high school librarian who has spent most of her life in New York City. The youngest of three children, she grew up in a nonobservant Jewish home. "When I was thirteen," Elaine recalls, "my family took a summer trip to Canada's rural province of New Brunswick. One afternoon we were on a leisurely drive. The weather was somewhat humid. My brother and sister were dozing next to me on the back seat, and my parents were talking quietly to each other about something. As I gazed out the window, I suddenly saw a wide river opening up into a seemingly infinite bay or ocean.

"The scene's grandeur overwhelmed me. The surprising and dramatic expanse of water reminded me of infinity, of the universe, and of God. Somehow I felt a kind of pride that I was the only one in the car who had glimpsed infinity: that great body of water, disappearing suddenly over the horizon, past the shorelines receding on either side of us. I felt a special connection to God.

"It was an intense and unforgettable moment, but I also

experienced a sense of insignificance as a human. I was attracted to the scene by its awesome beauty and simplicity: the simplicity of eternity."

Elaine comments, "The seeds of my entire outlook on life were planted in me that day. In retrospect, I only wish that I had shared my thoughts with my parents and siblings, and not felt superior to them because of my experience. Remembering it still gives me a sense of life's harmony and fulfillment: how life flows naturally to its end, to join in Infinity. The Eternal Presence is always with us."

In the English Countryside

James is a fifty-three-year-old biology teacher who has spent his entire life in England. A wildlife and music enthusiast, James recalls: "My first mystical experience—out of perhaps two or three during my lifetime—occurred when I was about six. We lived in Nottingham at the time, and one summer's day we were traveling on holiday to either the Derbyshire Peak District or rural Snowdonia, in Wales.

"Our car was small, and we were moving along a high road with a view over open countryside to our right. The air was not very clear, either hazy or misty. I caught sight of a small hill or a large rock with vegetation growing on it, projecting upward out of the haze. The base of the rock, along with the surrounding countryside, was not visible in any detail, but I have the impression that it may have been heather-covered moors.

"Suddenly, and without warning, I was filled with a kind of ecstasy, a great peace that filled my mind to the exclusion of all else. I suppose it lasted only a minute or so, but it made an indelible imprint on my consciousness.

"At the time, I associated the ecstatic experience with the specific *place*, and on at least three later summer holidays I eagerly looked out for the site as we drove by. Each time, I was sure the tremendous experience would be repeated. But I never recognized the place again—possibly because we subsequently took different routes, but more likely because I had failed to realize that the experience didn't come from the attributes of the place, but rather from my own mind.

"To this day," observes James, "that early experience is important because it gave me a taste of the peace that's possible in prayer and in the Quaker Meeting for Worship. The sense of ecstasy is usually lacking there, but the stillness is all the more powerful for that."

Embrace with the World

Vicki is a forty-seven-year-old office manager who has spent most of her life in New York City. The oldest of four children, she grew up in an abusive family. "My connectedness to nature is what inwardly sustained me," Vicki emphasizes. "Trees, plants, oceans, stars, the moon and sky were universes I could merge with. I would lose myself in contemplating, or swimming or climbing outdoors."

She particularly remembers: "One summer's day, when I was about ten, I went to the beach. With a large blanket covering the sand beneath me, I was lying on my stomach, arms outstretched into the warm air. Suddenly I had a flashing vision or sensation that I was embracing and being embraced by the entire globe of Earth. I felt so wonderful and happy that the joyous memory uplifted me for years to come."

Vicki comments: "I'm convinced that my survival, both emotionally and physically, was the result of these early experiences with nature. I know of many other incest survivors who furthermore believe that their abuse forced them to reach for other planes of existence. Perhaps this has also been true for me, though I'm not sure."

Clearing in the Woods

Rose is a seventy-six-year-old Hungarian émigré living in southern California. She came to the United States at the age of five. Three years later her mother suddenly died. "It was a tremendous blow to me. My whole life went into an upheaval, and I missed my mother very much. We ended up living with different families for a while," Rose recalls. "None of them ever lived the religion they were always shoving at me, and I was nearly an agnostic by the time I was almost twelve.

"I don't remember much about my father, except that he always petted my hair and said, 'You're my little girl.' That made me feel less lonely.

"One particular summer, my father sent me to a sleep-away camp for girls. I didn't make friends easily and felt lonely there much of the time. One sunny day, while all the other girls went to the lake for a swim, I walked into the woods. I came to a clearing and sat down by a tree stump.

"Sitting quietly, I was really trying to sort things out in my mind. Suddenly I became aware of what I can describe only as an awesome Presence around me. I was startled and overwhelmed, and I looked around. No one was there. I then experienced a tremendous warmth and love—beyond anything I could have conceived. Even then, though I was very negative about formal religion, I clearly thought, 'If there is a God, this has to be it.'

"As quickly as the episode occurred, it faded away," Rose

comments. "I've spent the rest of my life looking for such a beautiful Presence: in houses, in people, in places of worship. I've never found it. Yet I never again felt so alone in the world.

"Many years later, I found a spiritualist church where I could ask questions, and there I got answers. My experience in the summer woods is still clear in memory and has been an important influence through my entire life."

The Pulsating Sun

Diane is a forty-three-year-old music teacher/artist who has spent most of her life in Toronto. The older of two children, she grew up in a nominally United Church family. Diane recalls: "When I was very young, my neighborhood was mainly rural. It consisted of a small cluster of houses in a farm setting, backing onto a ravine filled with wondrous natural things.

"One day in early spring I was sitting quietly in our living room. I was just looking out at the world through a large bank of windows facing east. It was a beautiful day, and I felt happy and content. I must have been about three.

"As I looked at the dazzling blue sky, I saw the sun reflected in the window glass. Suddenly and with enormous joy, I felt the faraway sun to be 'pulsating' like a giant breathing heart in the sky. I was totally at one with the sun and wholly immersed in its living breath. I became aware of the life force that courses through all things, and I felt part of it.

"I don't know how long I sat there, transfixed and transformed by this experience," Diane continues. "At the time, I didn't even think of it as special or unusual. Later on, I became aware that other people couldn't relate to my description of what I had felt and tried dismissing it in a subtle way.

"But ever since that day, I've always sought the sun's life-giving light and have delighted in sitting or standing within it. As each day begins I find myself looking for signs of the sun: the light playing upon our bedroom wall, the shadows of leaves dancing along the windowsill. I've even come to regard the sun and the earth as living beings.

"Not long ago," Diane remarks, "I saw on a science program that scientists had excitedly discovered that the sun has a regular, measurable pulse or beat. Then, I just smiled to myself. It was something I had known for a long time."

New England Dawn

Suzanne is a thirty-seven-year-old psychotherapist and former music teacher living in central Connecticut. The younger of two children, she grew up in a nonreligious family in the Boston suburbs. At the age of nine, Suzanne underwent a mystical experience while on a Girl Scout camping trip on the Massachusetts seacoast.

"I awoke very early in the morning," Suzanne recalls, "feeling a strange compulsion to leave my tent in the darkness and make my way to the water's edge. Everyone else, including the counselors, was still sound asleep. I sat myself down, alone on the sandy shore, and silently watched the horizon.

"The sun was just coming up, as on any ordinary day, but my awareness suddenly became altered. I saw the light arising from the ocean in slow-moving, distinct particles, and I sat in awe as they combined in shifting patterns of many colors.

"By the time the sun had completely shown itself, I was transported by feelings that were overwhelming and wordless. They involved what I might now describe as a sense that everything fit together perfectly, that the world was fine in every way—and that life itself was a thing of wonder and magic.

"At the time," Suzanne comments, "I believed that all this was something that everyone—particularly adults—was aware of. I therefore felt that I had just been 'let in' on a great secret, and I kept the vision until I returned home from the camping trip. Then I excitedly tried explaining to my mother about the wonderful sunrise that I had seen. Her casual, almost bored reply was: 'Yes, dear, sunrises are beautiful.'

"Of course, I had been hoping for an explanation about the meaning of my experience and felt very disappointed by my mother's lack of understanding. Because I loved and respected her a great deal, I was puzzled by her indifferent reaction. Being only nine years old, I could find no words to explain my dazzling experience to her, and I decided to keep it to myself. But I also began to fear that there was something wrong with me.

"Somehow, though, I trusted my intuition. I knew that I had come into contact with something that no one in my suburban life had ever mentioned. A few years passed, and my search for the meaning of my experience led me on a 'spiritual journey' and eventually into Zen Buddhism.

"There my teacher convinced me that my sunrise experience might not be 'wrong' but something very true and real and shared by others. Not long after, while I was practicing Zen meditation, my childhood memory returned with great intensity, and I was finally able to recognize the spiritual encounter for what it was. I also felt sorrow for the little girl who had been enraptured and then made to feel such needless doubt.

"But I remain thankful for the experience, especially for the seed it planted in my consciousness, which grew in silence and darkness for nearly thirty years until the present. I am forever grateful for that opening-up to the truth of the world and of reality.

"Through practicing Zen, I have come to realize that my mystical episode can return with every moment: in a drop of water, a dirty dish, a glimpse of smile."

Nova Scotia Seascape

"I grew up on the seacoast of Nova Scotia and vividly experienced a delight in nature," relates Edward, a sixty-nine-year-old Protestant minister living in central Canada. "I had a strong sense of the numinous—and warmth and peace—that accompanied some of nature's moods. I felt let down with the world of people, their insensitivity to the beauty that was so real to me.

"At times I felt that the world was bleak and empty, devoid of purpose: that there had been a happiness somewhere that I had lost and for which I was searching. Much later, when I studied religious mysticism, I wondered if these longings were not buried memories of higher planes of life I had left to enter this world.

"One peak experience stands out in my memory," Edward recollects. "I had been sick and awoke one morning immersed in the most wonderful happiness I had ever known. Never before or since have I felt so happy. It seemed that a 'voice' spoke to me, though not in an audible way. What it said was, in effect, 'You will come here some day, but *not yet*.' This experience made a deep impression on me. I did share it with a few people in the ensuing years, but kept it mostly to myself.

"Another mystical experience came when I was a teenager in high school. It was September, and I was walking home from school some three miles through the Nova Scotia countryside. I still don't know exactly what triggered it, but I came to feel tremendously elated, and then euphoric. Simultaneously, the entire world seemed to be suffused with a tremendous light. I remember how at the walk's end, the light faded and passed into what the poet Wordsworth aptly called 'the light of common day.'

"I have spent over forty years in the ministry," Edward concludes, "and have often preached during Christmastime on 'The Lost Sense of Wonder.' I have often talked with children and been awed by their genuineness and responsiveness to spiritual matters. The mystic sense hasn't left me, and I still have the yearning to know and experience God more fully."

Swiss Forest Vision

Herbert is a thirty-five-year-old man who has spent most of his life in Basel, Switzerland. "I was about age six, one sunny spring day before Easter," he recalls, "and was eagerly searching for the nest of the Easter Bunny. I came to a place called the Little Oak Forest, a small forest of leafy trees. At its edges were tall oaks, and a brook with a waterfall about two meters high that crossed this little forest.

"In the middle of the forest there was a clearing. As I stepped into it, I was suddenly overwhelmed by the greenness of the overhanging young leaves and the lush meadow shining under a brilliant sun. I experienced an indescribable state of happiness, with an intense feeling of beauty, fullness, and perfection.

"Several years later," Herbert recollects, "I was in another Swiss forest on a hot summer's day. As I slowly walked along,

I saw a bird's feathers lying on the ground. They resembled stripes of blue, white, and black. Their beauty was so overpowering that I lost awareness of everything around me for what seemed like a long time."

Herbert comments, "Later, I used to come frequently to this forest in hopes of discovering those feathers again. But I never did. Both of these forest experiences have inspired me greatly over the years."

Winter Glade in British Columbia

Catherine is an eighty-five-year-old former schoolteacher living in Dorset, England. She grew up in Canada's pastoral province of British Columbia, the youngest of four children in an Anglican family. "It was the winter of my ninth year," she recalls, "and the snow had fallen all day long. When at last we were released from school, it had stopped snowing, but low clouds warned of further falls to come. Several inches must have been added since morning, for when I reached our field gate into the wood, the bottom latch was buried under snow.

"There was a small glade at the further side of the road. A stream ran through it and disappeared under a log bridge on its way to pastures beyond. I stopped, listening, when I reached the bridge. There was no sound of running water. The stream had frozen.

"The sky and everything around me were gray, except for a few green patches among the conifers. The temperature was certainly subfreezing. It must have been near sunset, but the western sky was hidden by trees. Home lay to the north, where the sky was darkest. I should have hurried on. Yet I stopped, regardless of the cold, beside the ice-bound stream.

"Then, quite rapidly," Catherine remembers, "a change took place. It began as a rift in the clouds overhead that widened to reveal blue sky.

"Like a morning-glory flower opening to the sun, the whole glade became lit with an unimaginable radiance. Bare branches sketched blue patterns across the snow. Icicles hanging from the bridge shone with silver and many shades of green. The glade was vivid, yet serene—poised in stillness, yet dazzlingly alive. It invoked in me a deep sense of worship. I whispered: 'Oh God, it's so lovely. Thank you for letting me see it.'

"How long the radiance in the wood lasted, I don't know—long enough to confirm my belief in God. And long enough, when at last it faded, for me to feel so stiff with cold that my legs were like ice blocks when I moved away.

"It's difficult to see through driving snow, and our house was almost invisible until I reached it. As I stamped my boots on the back veranda, my sister called me to hurry up, and I stumbled through the doorway. At our meal, I looked with somehow new-sighted eyes at my family seated around the dinner table. I experienced a new awareness about long-familiar things I had taken for granted. I had been shown tremendous beauty, which is a kind of love, and I was conscious in a new way about how much I loved my family."

In retrospect, Catherine observes: "The experience influenced me deeply and helped me through the hard times that soon followed, including my brother's combat in World War I and my mother's subsequent illness. Most directly, the episode in the glade propelled me into a more responsible state of childhood. It remains sharp in my memory, though I wasn't able to share it with anyone until many years later. At the time, I couldn't possibly have expressed what it meant to me. Even now, words fall far short of visual and spiritual memory."

The Humble Sequoias

Patricia is a thirty-five-year-old contract administrator living in southern California. An only child, she grew up Catholic in suburban Chicago. "My parents and I traveled west each summer," Patricia recalls, "and the trip through rural Nevada, Texas, and California always affected me very deeply. I would imagine with great intensity how the area looked when only Native Americans lived there and when the vast landscape was still unspoiled and pure.

"I was seven years old when I first saw the giant sequoias in California, and they exerted an intense effect on me. Even though they were extremely large, they appeared very humble and gentle to my youthful eyes. Somehow they seemed to cry out for help, and I felt a sense of love for them. It was as though they mourned the loss of each other sequoia tree destroyed by fire, as we humans would mourn the loss of a loved one.

"To me, the sequoias offered in their majesty a perfect example of how to offer oneself to God—as if to say, 'Do as you may with me, I am yours entirely through love.' "

Big Bend National Park

Michelle is a thirty-four-year-old dance therapist and program administrator living in southern Texas. She has been a professional dancer and has taught at high school and college levels. The middle-born of five children in a Catholic family, Michelle grew up in Houston.

"I was in the Girl Scouts for eight years," she recalls, "just so I could go camping. I loved being outdoors. When I was about thirteen, our Girl Scout troop made a summer trip to

Big Bend National Park. It was the first time that I had ever been there.

"I quietly awoke in the early morning, walked away from the camp, and sat on a boulder. No one else was awake yet, and the air was clear and still. I looked up and watched the flight of a big bird, probably a vulture. It glided on the air.

"Suddenly I felt totally transfixed. Time simply stopped. Nothing else existed. I was one with the bird and the sky as I sat on the boulder. Apparently, one of my Girl Scout friends who then saw me had to call my name repeatedly—and even became worried—in order to break the deep meditative state I was in.

"There were other times as a child," Michelle remembers, "in which I felt 'at one' with nature—whether it was relating to a flower, listening to the babble of a brook, gazing at a distant mountain range, or taking in the night sky.

"My main priority now is to bring this spirituality into my work in dance therapy. I have spent time with a Native American tribe in Mexico and researched their religion for my master's thesis on cross-cultural dance. I have also had profound experiences as an adult involving the Virgin of Guadalupe in Mexico, and regard Her as my protector."

Baltic Sea Ecstasy

"In the summer, our family would vacation at the Baltic Sea," fondly recalls Helga, a seventy-one-year old anthropology professor in California. An only child, she grew up in Berlin and was nominally raised as a Lutheran. "One day when I was four, I found myself standing at the beach, alone. The sea touched the sky. Breathing with the waves, I entered their rhythm. Suddenly there was a channeling of energy: the sun, the wind, the sea were going right through me.

"A door opened, and I *became* the sun, the wind, and the sea. There was no 'I' anymore. 'I' had merged with everything else. All sensory perceptions had become one. Sound, smell, taste, touch, shape—all melted into a brilliant light. The pulsating energy went right through me, and I was part of this energy.

"My parents found me transfixed on the beach and thought that I had suffered a heat stroke. So they kept me in bed, in the dark, for a couple of days. This gave me time to return to ordinary life.

"As a preschool child," Helga comments, "I didn't know what to do with this vision. There was no one with whom I could talk about it, since people would think I was crazy. However, in adulthood, whenever I've had a similar experience, I intuitively remember the first time. I've always been able to recall the light that enveloped and penetrated me. In this way, the episode at the Baltic Sea became a spiritual 'measuring rod' as to whether a later vision was genuine or just a fiction of my imagination."

Today Helga remains active as a scholar and teacher of comparative religion. With a special interest in shamanism and meditative techniques, she comments: "The surge of energy that swept through me sixty-seven years ago has continued to carry me. It reminds me that I will always be in the middle of the stream as long as I keep the memory alive."

Lake Michigan Beachfront

Judith is a fifty-six-year-old tour operator who lives in Phoenix, Arizona. The only child of divorced parents, she grew up in a conventional Presbyterian home in Michigan. "I was painfully shy, sensitive, and introspective by nature," Judith recalls, "and spent a great deal of time alone. During the wartime summer of 1943, when I was eight, my mother and I vacationed at an old family homestead in a wooded—and still wild—area that fronted on the beach at Lake Michigan.

"Most of my free time I spent near or in the water, which was then clear and lovely. As the summer days passed, I was gradually learning to trust the water to support my floating body.

"One day I was playing alone as usual while my mother watched me from the house. I was amusing myself by floating face down at the water's edge, and allowing the waves' gentle motion to carry me slowly back and forth. It was close to an area where a small stream entered the main body of water. Open-eyed in the cool water, I lay watching the sunlight reflect and sparkle off the tiny, water-polished stones. I continued gazing and began noticing how the pebbles washed back and forth, right below me, at the shallow edge where the water met the land. I was taking deep breaths and holding them for as long as possible.

"Suddenly," Judith remembers vividly, "I shifted into a state of awareness that was far more acute than usual, and I experienced a powerful sense of the beauty of the stones, the sparkling light, and the water's fluid motion. I experienced such an intense joy that I could hardly endure it.

"After an unknown period of time while my euphoria intensified, I sensed what I was seeing in terms of a larger context: the land meeting the water, mineral density meeting less dense fluid. Then I felt the Great Lake as being part of a wonderful, wonderful phenomenon: the Earth. I became aware of its spherical nature and experienced it as an exquisite blue-and-white sphere moving among vast, vast other bodies of light. It was a startling image for me, because books during that (pre-Space Age) era invariably depicted the Earth as green, or brown-and-green."

Today Judith has a strong interest in nature and organizes tours designed to awaken our innate sense of wonder. She comments: "I have certainly experienced ups and downs over the years, like everyone else. But since the episode on the shore, a part of me has always felt conscious of the 'real' situation and is never shaken by anything. My commitment to spirituality and the 'Mysteries' has remained the most powerful and unwavering force in my life."

3

Backyard Visions

The great lesson from the true mystics is that the sacred is in the ordinary, that it is to be found in one's daily life, in one's neighbors, friends, and family, and in one's back-yard.

—ABRAHAM MASLOW

As vividly seen in chapter 2, nature's grandeur in its different forms has the capacity to elicit great joy during our early years. Whether occurring on a wild mountainside, on an expansive seashore, or in a serenely rolling countryside, these experiences share a common sense of awe and even homage regarding our natural world.

Yet as children (and adults) we are also capable of being tremendously moved and uplifted by nature's day-to-day constancy. As the following reminiscences indicate, the backyard of childhood is often a place of wonder. For some of us it had a coziness that helped us to feel at home in the world. We felt secure and happy there. For others it became a true refuge, or sanctuary, where quiet and peacefulness reigned in an otherwise untrustworthy existence.

Can a child fall in love with a familiar tree? A garden plot? A stolid boulder? In our contemporary society, these emotional memories are probably suppressed—perhaps at high personal cost—among many men and women. Undoubtedly, many of us feel a sense of vague longing for a true bond that we no longer consciously remember.

Perhaps some of the accounts that follow will gently awaken your own childhood love for nature's everyday companionship. Most immediately, the question then arises: What moments of delight and rapture are we missing that might still be awaiting in our ordinary backyard?

Montana Homestead

Gloria is an eighty-year-old retired public health administrator living in rural Washington. An only child, she was born into a Unitarian family in rural Texas. Gloria recalls: "When I was seven, we first moved out to a homestead on a ranch in Montana. We were situated on the divide between the Big Powder River and the Little Powder River. Roads were difficult and travel was usually by team and wagon or horseback. Our first house there was a one-room log cabin. It had been built near a little spring beside which grew many wild shrubs and pine trees.

"One morning I was alone with my grandmother and trying to sew something. Somehow I accidentally jabbed the needle into the palm of my hand. I cried out in throbbing pain. Grandma immediately offered to extract the sewing needle, but I was afraid of her shaky hands and insisted that my mother should perform the removal instead. Then Grandma promised me a dime if I'd let her extract it. Before I could reply, mother walked in.

"Hearing about the financial offer, she angrily scolded me for being 'spoiled.' I tried denying the charge, but to no avail. Feeling deeply hurt and misunderstood," Gloria remembers, "I went off into our backyard and wandered to one of the huge old pine trees. I sat down beside it, with my back pressing against its bark, and gradually became aware of its surging strength. In some undefinable way, I felt the pine's life energy moving against my back, and I sensed the long years the tree had stood there.

"Simultaneously I experienced for the first time a profound sense of myself as truly separate from my mother—and my hurt feelings instantly melted away. Instead I felt connected to a vast, natural power: a calm, quiet, living presence that was just there and immensely comforting to me.

"From that time on," Gloria comments, "I would often go and sit against that pine tree, not quite knowing why, but drawn intensely to its being. It radiated a quality of timelessness beyond my personal worries, and it became a constant source of comfort in my life—so much so that, years later, when I first earned money from school teaching, I bought a camera and made a special trip just to photograph that tree. I particularly liked one shot and kept it in an old cardboard folder for decades.

"Finally, when I was in my forties, I decided that if that pine tree possessed such meaning and memory for me, then I certainly ought to have the photograph properly matted and framed. This I did. For nearly forty years the pine tree photograph has hung on my study wall, and it still remains my daily link between heaven and earth."

Pond Life

Jackie is a forty-four-year-old biology teacher living in a suburb of New York City. The third-born of seven, she grew up in Indiana in a Congregationalist family.

"One spring day when I was eleven," Jackie recalls, "my

older brother Steve took me along, for the first time, on a hike to a pond in the woods outside of town. I was excited to be with him, especially since I was physically small for my age and rarely involved in hiking or athletic activities.

"We walked down a long dirt road until we came to a fence. Nailed to a tree was a sign: No Trespassing, Violaters Will Be Prosecuted.

"Though I reacted timidly, Steve was certainly undeterred by the warning. He immediately climbed the fence, and after a moment's hesitation I quickly followed. Below the trees I could see last year's oak leaves, now floating in a huge puddle created by the recent spring rain. The water was a pale brown color from the dark leaves.

"Gazing into the nearby pond was like inspecting crystal, it was so clear. The sun's light was so bright. All the colors seemed brighter than in ordinary life. Then I saw the tadpoles. They were the color of black velvet and looked like little oval heads with tails that shimmered like black ribbons fluttering in the wind. They clustered around the puddle's edge, and wriggled incessantly with energy.

"There were fairy shrimp there, too," remembers Jackie, "pale orange and feathery, swimming on their backs with their many legs moving rhythmically, their eyes little black dots on their faces. They lived only in spring, from the time of the rain until the pond dried up in the summer's heat. I wondered where they stayed all the rest of the year, when the woods didn't have a pond. How could a life be so short and yet keep returning dependably every April?

"That entire afternoon I felt entranced by all the pond life. I was irretreviably, forever in love with the crystal pond and the feeling of magic there."

Jackie attributes her later decision to major in biology and become a science teacher to this intense encounter with nature.

She comments: "It also gave me a clear picture of universal energy—light—being present, of creation being everywhere, all the time. The experience clarified my feeling of awe about nature's beauty and how I hadn't valued it sufficiently before."

In the Rose Garden

Phyllis is a sixty-two-year-old retired office manager living in southern California. The oldest of three sisters, she grew up in a nonreligious household in Pittsburgh. "My parents gave me very little warmth and not much personal freedom," Phyllis recalls. "I was quite an unhappy girl, but sometimes found solace in my friendships.

"One spring day, when I was five years old, I was visiting my grandmother and playing in her backyard. She had a lovely rose garden that she carefully tended. I sat on the grass and played near it, and then decided to walk over and look more closely at the roses.

"As I did so, I suddenly felt God's presence in an almost overpowering way. The 'trigger' could partly have been the sheer beauty of the roses, but something else must have lifted my being into a new realm of awareness. The sensation probably lasted only a few minutes at most. But as a result, I became a lifelong believer in God.

"Fifty-seven years have passed," Phyllis comments, "and I still remember this experience quite clearly."

Moon and Stream

Corrine is a forty-seven-year-old farmer who has spent most of her life in rural Missouri. The third of four children, Corrine grew up in a nominally Catholic home. "When I was very young," she recalls, "less than four, because we were still living in our first house, I had an experience with the full moon.

"I was lying in my bed. It was wintertime and must have been late at night, for our house was silent. A large tree outside my window was bare of leaves. I noticed that the moon was large and luminous through the branches. As I lay on my bed in the moonlight, I suddenly felt myself being absorbed into the light—drawn up, in a sense, into the moon.

"The experience was very odd, and yet pleasant. In retrospect, it was as though I became entranced by the moon and entered a timeless moment of oneness with everything.

"Several years later," Corrine remembers, "I used to spend hours by myself sitting on a large rock at the edge of a stream near our home. I would engage in 'silent gazing,' as I called it, just staring at the moving water and the sunlight rippling through it.

"Such experiences gave me a very intense feeling about God and self. As an adult, I've sought to recapture that childhood closeness through living in the country and practicing daily meditation."

Seeing the Big Picture

Madeline is a fifty-six-year-old retired schoolteacher who has spent most of her life in the New York City area. The third-born of four children, she grew up in a Catholic family.

"As a youngster, I was nervous and overly sensitive," Madeline recalls. "I constantly whined about how other people—mostly family members, I guess—were hurting my feelings. I would always feel victimized and cry easily.

"Then, one spring night when I was about fourteen, I was gazing out my bedroom window as usual. It was very still outside. Suddenly I felt transfixed by the sight of the street-lamp's soft light shining through the leafy, green trees on the sidewalk.

"In that moment I experienced a tremendous feeling of peace different from anything before in my life. It was as though I were looking at my entire life from a great height or distance and could see everything in a detached way.

"It's difficult to put into words: it was a total sense of calmness and acceptance about my life and its concerns, that there was no need to worry. With complete serenity, I felt aware of my life as a small part of something much greater, and my sense of constant victimization suddenly disappeared."

Madeline concludes, "It's not as if I never had any worries after this experience, but it did change my deepest outlook about life. In retrospect, I feel as though I had seen the Big Picture, and it was immensely comforting to me."

One with the Wind

"I was about ten when a special event occurred in my life," recalls Martha, a sixty-year-old high school English teacher living in southern California. "I had a younger sister, and we grew up in a middle-class Catholic family in the Chicago area. Several blocks from home, there was a section where very large old trees lined the streets.

"On this particular day, a storm was clearly coming in. The winds steadily increased and seemed to be descending upon the earth. My every sense was focused on the drama of nature.

"As I walked through the area, I could hear the wind's approach. I watched as the topmost branches of the old trees began to weave and toss. The wind's energy was being transmitted down to the ground and roots through branches, limbs, and tree trunks.

"I could hear the voices of the trees as they responded to the wind, and I felt a kinship with them. All of a sudden, I had the intense sensation that the wind knew *I* was there. I had a tremendous feeling of belonging, of at-one-ment, and great exhilaration."

Martha never shared this intense experience with her parents or sister, for fear of being misunderstood or ridiculed. "I suppose I became interested in the natural world in a way that I expected no one to understand rationally. Maybe that's why I later turned to painting and poetry as means of communicating." Much later in life, after moving to California, Martha again had the intense experience that the "wind knew my name."

Today Martha is married and has a daughter in her mid-twenties. "I attend no church," she explains. "But I pray and meditate; I read spiritual books and try to live gently. I'm in search of a larger God."

San Francisco Sunlight

Donna is a forty-seven-year-old woman living in Sacramento. The older of two children born to a Catholic father and nondenominational mother, she grew up in San Francisco.

"One spring day, when I was about seven," Donna recalls, "I was outside playing happily in the late afternoon. I looked toward the sun. Clouds were slowly floating across it, and the rays beaming out from behind them were glorious. I became utterly entranced with the whole vision.

"I had the intense feeling that God was somehow speaking to me through this scene. At that instant, I just knew that *God was in everything* and that *everything was a part of God.* I felt awed by the whole experience, but never told anyone about it.

"Interestingly, before this beautiful episode occurred," comments Donna, "I had longed to attend church and to know God better. Even before I was introduced to church or Sunday school, I felt a special closeness with nature."

Autumn Ozark Afternoon

Elizabeth is a forty-eight-year-old educational counselor living in rural Idaho. "Growing up in the Ozark Mountains of southern Missouri, I loved being outdoors. I spent many hours with my brothers and sisters playing cowboys-and-Indians games, and just generally running about. I was the middle of ten children, and I always had someone to look up to, look down on, or just be with.

"The day I vividly remember was in the fall of my sixth year. It was still quite warm, and the sun was shining through the many colors of leaves still clinging stubbornly to the trees. I had gone about a mile away from my house for a walk. It was the first time I had gone so far all by myself.

"I remember the sound of the leaves softly crackling beneath my feet, like little angels whispering secrets about me in a special language. The rays of sunlight filtered through the remaining leaves on the trees, warming my skinny arms and seeming to move with me as I made my journey. The feeling I had was one of total well-being, mastery, and great confidence."

Elizabeth comments: "This was such a simple little adventure, yet its memory has uplifted me many times throughout my life. Whenever I think of it, I am filled with peace and confidence. As a young child, I certainly didn't know anything about the term 'peak experience.' But as I think back, it seems clear this must surely have been one."

Merging with a Rainbow

Carolyn is a fifty-three-year-old woman living in Springfield, Illinois. She recalls that at the age of eight or nine, "early one June, school had just let out and there was a very pleasant summer rain. After the shower ended, I went back outside my house to play. The sun began to shine again, and everything was sparkling. Much to my surprise and delight, I saw in the sky a vivid rainbow forming, its base seeming to be only twenty feet away.

"I remembered the old tale about the pot of gold at the rainbow's end, but even at that age I knew it was not real. I put down my doll and walked right into the rainbow's prism of colors. I felt totally transfixed as I walked back and forth, changing colors. I knew that I was one with all. It was an intensely emotional event for me. I stood there for a long while, and when the colors began to fade, I felt a deep sadness."

Carolyn comments: "After more than forty years, I can still experience the same oneness whenever I see a rainbow. The same emotions rise up: deep spiritual feelings, a sense of eternity, and a sense of unity with the God force. Of all the events that I experienced during my childhood years, this particular one had the greatest emotional and spiritual impact upon me. It still does."

The Doll in the Poplar Grove

A seventy-five-year-old retiree living in central Florida, Gladys is active with the Quakers and interested in Jungian psychology. "I grew up in Peoria, Illinois," she recalls, "where I was the youngest of four children. My family was only nominally involved with the Congregational church and never discussed religion very much.

"One day, when I was about four years old, I was standing alone in our backyard. It held eight large silver-leaf poplars, with bark that was black-and-white.

"I held a tiny china doll in my hand, and then placed the doll on a piece of the bark. Suddenly, in a way that I still can't explain, I experienced the most wonderful, blazing feeling of happiness. I felt a euphoric awareness that *'This world is wonderful!'*

"Seventy years have passed," Gladys concludes. "Though I've certainly had sadness in my life, this experience was like a beam of sunshine that seemed to be within everything: a joyful place to which I could always return."

Twigs and Intuition

Kathy is a thirty-nine-year-old executive secretary who has spent most of her life in the New York City area. Raised as a

Catholic, Kathy recalls: "When I was a young child, I was strongly attracted to sticks shaped like a Y. I would call them *magic* and 'bless' myself and my friends by waving them with careful gestures. It wasn't until my adulthood that I learned that such sticks have for centuries been used as dowsing rods.

"By my early teens I had done a lot of thinking about life and death and human existence. As a result, I developed a personal understanding of God as an 'energy' rather than what my religious teachers were insisting. This was years before I did any reading about mysticism. In fact," Kathy comments, "Many things that, as a child, I intuitively felt to be true only much later did I read about as an adult."

The Living Earth

"My spiritual journey began early in my childhood," recalls Dennis, a thirty-five-year-old man living in rural North Carolina. "It was hard for me to make friends, as I was easily intimidated by others and stuttered horribly whenever I tried speaking. My speech impediment caused me to feel emotionally fragile and isolated from others.

"Because of this," Dennis comments, "I would usually play alone, deeply engrossed in the imaginings of my mind. On the farmland where we lived, I would concentrate for hours on little square patches of earth and watch with fascination at all the bustling life and activity that was occurring there. Plants and animals radiated an aura of aliveness, and I often felt that I was simply part of a great Whole.

"When I was a bit older, I would leave our house and sit quietly in the woods. I experienced many inner guides to peace: the musical wind in the trees, the songs of insects and birds, even the far-off noise of civilization.

"As a result of these encounters, I learned that each of us has a silent voice that speaks with God. All we have to do is allow it to happen."

Lesson of the Butterfly

Kate is a fifty-two-year-old cosmetologist who has lived most of her life in rural New Hampshire. Raised in the Protestant faith, Kate recalls: "When I was about ten, we had a mailbox at the end of the road. It was my daily responsibility to bring in the mail. One day in early spring, I discovered a cocoon in the back of the mailbox.

"I didn't touch the cocoon, but I was very curious and carefully watched it every day. A few weeks passed, and one morning the mailbox had caterpillars in it! It wasn't long after that several beautiful butterflies together flew out on a bright, sunny afternoon.

"Seeing their swift flight into the air affected me deeply. Somehow I immediately knew that here was an important lesson from nature: life goes on and on for all of us. We may not look the same each time, but nonetheless we are reborn."

Kate also recollects: "We had two large maple trees that I used to watch from season to season. I would ponder their changes: new leaves to green, then colored leaves, then no leaves, and then new leaves again. Yet, amid these vivid changes, the trees were the same. Such observations always assured me that God had given us examples to see and know about. Because of these experiences, I have always felt a sense of closeness to Creation and its wonders."

Splendor in the Grass

Yvonne is a forty-seven-year-old woman living in Scotland who runs a small marketing business with her husband. "I don't remember how old I was," she recalls, "but I can be fairly sure that I was younger than eleven. I was lying on my stomach on the grass one sunny afternoon, beneath a tree in our garden, doing nothing and thinking about nothing in particular. Then I began watching the ants struggling to move small bits of leaf through the blades of grass.

"The ants had such difficulty in maneuvering themselves among the rather coarse, dry, and closely growing blades of grass that I was fascinated by their energy and determination regarding what seemed like a gigantic task.

"Suddenly my attention became so focused that I lost all sense of myself and my ordinary existence. I felt as though I were that world of ants, the brown terrain under their black legs, the obstacles in their path, the air enclosed by the green thickets reaching above them. Somehow I was fully merged with the ants' aliveness and purpose."

Yvonne remembers: "When the experience was over, I certainly felt surprised, but not really startled. It didn't occur to me that it might have been at all unusual. A few years passed, and in high school we were studying Wordsworth's 'Ode: Intimations of Immortality.' Then the full force of my experience came back to me, and I felt saddened to think that I might never have a similar one again.

"This episode has undoubtedly been the basis of my own ideas about God, and it has led me to my chief interests: watercolor painting of landscape scenes, and reading and writing poetry. Looking back, I think the experience was triggered by the combined effect of unusual concentration and absorption in a very relaxed atmosphere."

Awakening to Birds

Monique is a twenty-eight-year-old office manager living in Reno, Nevada. An only child, she grew up in Los Angeles with little formal religious training. Monique recalls: "One morning, when I was perhaps three years old, I awakened to the sounds of birds singing outside my bedroom window. I distinctly remember thinking as I awoke, 'I hope to wake up *every* morning to the sounds of birds!' Those were my exact words.

"I was a quiet and shy child," Monique comments. "Years later, I now regard the experience as something unusual, for I've always been drawn to nature more than to institutional religion. In fact, several months before that blissful awakening, I attended Easter Sunday services with my aunt and cousin. As we walked out of church, I held my aunt's hand and intensely felt, 'That's not the place for me!' "

Secure in the Woods

Brian is a thirty-six-year-old musician who has lived in southern New Jersey for most of his life. The younger of two brothers, he was exposed to little religious training. "When I was about three," Brian recalls, "my father had just finished constructing a beautiful home on about twenty acres of woodland. Unfortunately, the atmosphere within was anything but peaceful, because my parents fought continually. I felt very lonely.

"Yet I always loved being outside, and I would look with

longing at the tall pine trees that surrounded our backyard. One day I felt enough courage to slip away from my mother's watchful eye and walked alone into the woods. It was there that I found the joy I had been disappointedly seeking in my own family. The woods felt peaceful and loving, and there I felt really at home.

"I knew that my mother would be mad at me for having disappeared," Brian continues, "but as I kept walking deeper into the woods, the more wonderful it became. After exploring and talking happily with everything I could see, I lay down under a big pine tree. From its many-rooted base I could see straight up to the sky and feel its branches dancing with the wind. I knew that I was safe, and more than that, I felt loved by all that was around me. I felt connected to the plants, trees, animals, and even the insects, and I fell asleep surrounded by love.

"Sure enough, my mother was furious when I returned home," recollects Brian, "and I had no one with whom I could relate my experience. Nevertheless, it helped me to understand that I was in communication with God and that I should never lose sight of that fact. For me, it has taken years of spiritual searching to understand fully the natural simplicity and perfection of my childhood episode in the woods."

From a Bedroom Window

Hillary is a thirty-one-year-old elementary school teacher currently living in Nepal. The oldest of three children, she grew up in eastern Massachusetts in a Congregationalist family. "When I was eight," Hillary recalls, "I used to awaken early in the morning. Before I would open my bedroom door and walk downstairs, no one knew I was awake. This afforded me ample time to gaze out my bedroom window.

"The leafy street scene was always the same. The game that I invented for myself was to try finding something different or something that had changed since the last time I had looked. I would stare at the side of our neighbor's house for a long time, or look at the tree and its buds or the shaking of its leaves. I was fascinated by squirrels as they scurried up trees and jumped from branch to branch.

"I also loved to look at the bright patterns of snow or ice on my windowpane and to smell the fresh cold air blowing in where the windowsill wasn't very tight. After lying in bed and looking for a while in this way, I would get up, feeling wonderfully refreshed and calm."

Hillary comments: "I never talked to anyone about these experiences. Somehow it didn't seem appropriate. But they certainly motivated my interest in spirituality and nature. As an adult, I've come to adopt the Buddhist philosophy that all sentient beings want happiness, and I am therefore a vegetarian. Also, I try interacting with everyone in a positive way—in the words of one of my Buddhist teachers, 'to make others happy.'"

Backyard Bliss

Diana is a twenty-one-year-old musician living in Allentown, Pennsylvania. Raised as a Catholic in New York City, she was the second-born of four children. "We had a large and noisy family," Diana recalls, "and things were constantly hectic inside our house. In particular, my parents were always yelling at each other, and eventually they divorced.

"Our house had a fenced-in backyard, and when I was about six I discovered a wonderful spot inside the bushes. There I could sit comfortably on a branch and lean against the trunk. There was another branch where I could put my feet. The foliage was thick enough that I couldn't be seen, and my spot was behind our swimming pool, so no one could watch me enter or leave.

"I'd listen to the birds and enjoy the feel of the gently swaying branches beneath me, if there was a wind or strong breeze. I'd just relax and quietly let my thoughts wander. Often, if something was bothering me, or if I was puzzled, I'd think about it there in my backyard 'sanctuary' and find an answer."

Diana remarks: "It seemed as though I had a short visit with God each time I went to my special spot inside the bushes. It was as though I knew He could hear me there, and that if I listened closely enough I could hear Him too. The time I spent outdoors there always left me with a very strong sense of peace: with myself, nature, and everything."

4

Near-Death and Crisis Experiences

Even though I walk the valley of the shadow of death, I
fear no evil, for you are with me.
—PSALM 23:4

*I*N the preceding two chapters we have heard from people recounting uplifting childhood encounters with nature. Some of these were highly dramatic, others more quietly inspiring. Such varied accounts confirm the viewpoint about nature mysticism that has long been advocated by thinkers dating back to Blake and Wordsworth, and undoubtedly earlier.

Yet human life is inevitably filled with vicissitudes and sometimes even becomes a struggle for sheer physical survival. A vital question therefore arises: do we grow inwardly only from joyful occurrences, or can seemingly negative events too serve to awaken our higher strengths and sensitivities? Psychological researchers definitely believe so, for it is already well established that adults who undergo near-death phenomena often gain a new, more secure outlook on life. They feel more at peace with themselves and their surroundings. Sometimes, even if lacking any previous religious interest, they become drawn to sacred and mystical teachings.

Our exploration of childhood's "peaks" confirms this finding. As the following narratives reveal, some of us are able to trace our key spiritual moments to early confrontations with death, or more generally, to episodes of danger or crisis.

Coma in Germany

Ursula, a thirty-five-year-old mother of two children, has spent her entire life in Germany. She recalls: "On my fourth birthday I suffered a severe fall from a horse and landed on my head. My skull was fractured in several places, and I had hemorrhaging in my brain. I lay many days in a coma, and later I learned that the doctors had informed my parents, 'Your daughter has no chance of survival.'

"However, I can still remember that right after the accident, I stepped out of my body—feeling so light and carefree—into a tremendously expansive ocean of light. I was greeted by spiritual teachers who were humorous and seemed to know everything about me. They advised me that if I wanted to return to my body, it would need to be healthy when I was bigger, and that they would help me in the healing process. Then a determination was made for me to return to my body. The reversion was a very painful event.

"The body seemed small to me," Ursula recollects, "and it was a twisting-and-turning and here-and-there process. In the ensuing days, while I still lay in coma, I heard exactly what the doctors were saying about me: for instance, that if I survived, I would be retarded in my development. But I had the inner knowledge or wisdom that I would be fully healed.

"When I recovered from the coma, I felt a new ability to sense things about other people. I also felt very close to Jesus in a way that made me very secure and happy. This awareness had nothing to do with the church in my community, for the sermons there always stressed guilt and punishment. In fact, I often felt an urge to get up and bless the congregants around me."

Ursula comments: "When I reached the age of sixteen, I began to study world religions and philosophy. My mother was at first astonished and complained that I didn't seem interested in the matters of other girls my age. I began practicing meditation a great deal and in college greatly enjoyed my studies, especially drama training. There I once again found the bright side of life. Today I find my relationship with my two sons to be a constant source of spiritual enlightenment and joy. From the earliest age they have felt comfortable about discussing spiritual matters with me."

"Look to the Stars"

Audrey is a fifty-two-year-old music teacher living in a suburb of New York City. "At the age of three and a half," she recalls, "I was very ill with rheumatic fever and rheumatic arthritis. One night, as I sobbed uncontrollably from the terrible pain, my grandmother gently told me, 'Look up, and when the pain is bad, go to the stars.'

"Later that night I again felt excruciating pain and decided to follow her advice. I gazed at the stars, visible through my bedroom window. Suddenly I felt myself in the midst of a glowing, pulsating, slowly swirling light. I *knew* everything. I *was* everything. It was blissful beyond words. The next morning I felt immeasurably better, and my illness soon went away. I have never forgotten the experience."

Today Audrey has a strong interest in mysticism, including theosophy and the Kabbalah.

Basement Electrocution

Lenora is a thirty-eight-year-old woman who has lived in central Pennsylvania most of her life. The oldest of three children, Lenora was raised in a Catholic household. "One spring day when I was about eleven, I came home from school as usual. I was the only one home yet, as my parents and siblings had gone shopping. I took off my jacket and went down to the cellar. I was planning to wash out something, then noticed that the floor was flooded from the washing machine and tubs.

"I tried to mop up the floor, and I opened the drain for the water to run out. It was a big and time-consuming job for a little girl, but I tried to do my best. Still no one else had come home. I got most of the water cleaned up and then prepared to go upstairs and do my homework.

"I went to turn out the light over the old kitchen sink, forgetting that I was standing in a puddle of water and that my hands were wet. To my horror, I accidentally grabbed the lamp's neck instead of its switch. Instantly I felt a surging current of electricity running up my arm and into my heart.

"I had grabbed the light with my right hand and couldn't let go. I knew that I was going to die. I tried and tried to release my hand, but couldn't. I called out for help, though I knew that no one was home. My voice sounded different, and I was crying. I had the image of my parents coming home and finding me dead and electrocuted in the cellar, and I thought how horrible it would be to die this way.

"Then all of a sudden my hand was pushed or was pulled off the lamp's neck. I couldn't believe it. I wasn't dead. It wasn't my time to die. Someone had saved me. My body was wet and still tingling from the electricity, but I was okay.

"I never told my parents or anyone about this episode. I was afraid they would blame me for being stupid, which they did on many occasions. I had no one with whom I could share the experience.

"Today I'm very interested in religious teachings," Lenora concludes, "and though my family responsibilities are time-consuming, I talk to God and try to meditate every day."

Australian Near-Drowning

Kim is a thirty-year-old data-entry typist who has spent most of her life within suburban Melbourne, Australia. The youngest of four children, she grew up in a Methodist family.

"My story begins in the summer when I was about nine," Kim recalls. "As a child, my Christmas holidays were always spent with other family members at the beach. At the time, I didn't know how to swim. I usually just waded instead, and that was fine. One day I waded out too far. The sand bank on which I was walking suddenly dropped five feet.

"I lost my balance and fell down into the water, hard. I immediately felt sharp pain and found that I had wounded my leg. I panicked and began thrashing around in the water. Within a few seconds I no longer knew the right way up. Although I could see occasional flashes of daylight, I couldn't steady myself to break through the water's surface. Suddenly I felt myself gasping for air. I really thought that I was going to die, and I prayed to God to save me.

"Then a strange thing happened. A calm feeling engulfed me from head to foot. Even though my body was still thrashing around in the water, I found that my mind had calmed and was not panicked anymore. At that moment, I saw the figure of Jesus. He held his hand upright in a sign of peace and was surrounded by deep blue water.

"I said, 'Dear God, save me. I'll do anything you want of me. Only give me some signs along the way so that I'll know *what* you want of me.'

"I thanked God for listening. I remember repeating my thank-you several times, and then suddenly my cousin pulled me out of the water."

For the next three years Kim relived her experience almost nightly in her dreams. Sometimes she had this recurrent dream several times in the same night. "It was a difficult time for me. I was astounded that I had no one to turn to for help. All my life my parents had been there to guide me. After the near-drowning I realized that I had to take charge of my own life. I became withdrawn in my quest for inner knowledge and my reason for being alive.

"I stopped taking things for granted," Kim comments, "and instead started appreciating my surroundings more. I had a greater sense of right and wrong, good and bad. I took up gardening, embroidery, and listening to classical music. After the experience I also became more discerning about people. I could see an individual's true personality right away. I have learned to trust my first impressions, and am guided by the adage 'What you see is what you get.'

"This experience also made me more sensitive to other people's needs and less selfish. I had always believed in God," Kim reflects, "even before that experience. But it took several years to realize that my faith had deepened. When I see someone do an act of kindness, whether it be to another person, to an animal, or even to the earth, I feel all choked up. I often thank God for these acts and for many other simple things: the wind on my face, a thunderstorm, ants making a nest, birds having a bath, or a flower's opening. I know that everything has a reason for being. I thank God that I have taken the time to notice these things. I often look at these things as God's acts of kindness to us, and as reminders that He's there to help us.

"Through my near-drowning at age nine, I know that life is short. After that episode I also realized how precious life is. Death can come at any time, but I don't fear death. I was given a second chance at life, and at that age, I felt it was my duty to learn why and to do the best I could with my second chance."

The Sparrow of Hope

Lisa is a thirty-five-year-old woman living in the Los Angeles area. "I was born and raised in rural Maryland," she recalls, "and exposed to a lot of folklore and superstition. For example, if a bird flew into your windowpane and died, it meant someone close to you was going to die soon. As a baby I developed severe allergies, hay fever, and asthma, and I spent longer periods each summer confined to my bed.

"The summer of my eleventh birthday was the worst," Lisa recounts. "I spent nearly the entire time in bed except for many midnight trips to the hospital emergency room for a shot of adrenaline. I used to plan surprise 'trips' downstairs just to visit my family. But after taking nearly a half hour to walk down one flight of stairs, I would become so ill that I had to be carried back to bed.

"One hot, unpleasantly humid August afternoon, I heard a crash against my bedroom window. It was so loud that I thought the window had shattered. A small brown sparrow lay crumpled on the outer windowsill.

"Fear grabbed me as I realized that the sparrow was my 'life sparrow.' I knew everyone secretly expected me to die, but I didn't really believe it myself. As I watched the sparrow quietly lying there, I wondered whether dying wasn't such a terrible thing and whether I should accept it. I had already made my peace with God, but I had always felt that a major change was coming and that I had a lot to accomplish in life.

"All of a sudden the little sparrow began to twitch and move. It stood up on the windowsill, but seemed very disoriented. The sparrow sat there for a long time, as though thinking and gathering strength. Then it turned and stared right at me for the longest time. Abruptly the sparrow danced on the windowsill and pecked loudly at the glass. Finally it flew off.

"At that moment, I *knew* that I had been right all along and that I wouldn't die from my asthma condition. From that day onward, as subsequent medical examinations confirmed, my health showed a definite improvement. It followed the pattern of the little sparrow who awoke and recovered from the crash in my bedroom. Looking back, I feel that God gave me the hope I needed through creating this event in my life."

Near-Death in the Amusement Park

Jessica is a thirty-year-old woman living in southern California. She recalls: "One day, while I was of kindergarten age, I traveled with my sister and mother, along with a neighbor and her two children, to a local amusement park. I felt the occasion was special because I was wearing a lovely new dress.

"Eventually our attention was drawn to a ride called 'Crack the Whip.' It seemed that everyone had found a car and was already seated, but I was still trying to find a vacant seat. Finally I located one and started to climb in. I hadn't yet put both my legs into the car when suddenly the operator started up the ride and the machine began to move. I hopped around, not being able to get all the way in or all the way out.

"The ride began to gain speed, going faster and faster. I tried shouting for help, but no one heard me. I vividly remember falling into the center of the machinery and struggling to jump over the center bars. I obviously failed, for I abruptly lost consciousness."

Jessica continues: "My next recollection is that of an observer. I felt myself hovering from a position above the ground, and I clearly witnessed my small body caught in the machinery. Then an indeterminate time passed, and I found myself awakening in the arms of a strange man and asking for my mother. I was upset because my pretty new dress was ripped and covered with black grease and grime. I was taken by ambulance to the hospital, where I regained strength.

"It's hard to say precisely how my out-of-body experience affected me," concludes Jessica, "but I've been convinced since then that there's something more to human existence than meets the eye."

Near-Death in British Columbia

Emily is a forty-nine-year-old legal secretary living in Vancouver, Canada. The younger of two sisters, she was born into a Protestant family in western Canada. "One summer's day when I was about nine," Emily recalls, "I was rocking a raft up and down with a bunch of other kids in the Thompson River area of British Columbia. Suddenly the raft flipped over and somehow pinned me underneath it.

"Within a few seconds I must have started drowning. But I remember only a sense of instant surrender and relief. I felt myself entering into what seemed like a place of golden light where images of my life and universal, cosmic information were displayed to me. It was as though I were watching a movie screen, but I wasn't separate from it. I was both watching and participating, and my sense was one of perfection: a perfect, joyful state of just *being*.

"Then suddenly there was a feeling of inner acceleration. The next thing I knew I was scolding the people who were pumping the water out of me and saying to them, 'Leave me alone! I want to go back!'

As an adult, Emily attended several Buddhist meditation retreats, "where I found access to very much the same states of being through meditation. Also, my two teenage children have been my main spiritual teachers. They've helped me to know that I've come from bliss and will one day return to bliss."

Through the Windshield

Andrew is a forty-seven-year-old businessman who has spent most of his life in Cleveland, Ohio. The older of two brothers, he grew up in a Jewish family. "While driving at the age of seventeen," Andrew recalls, "I was hit by an oncoming car. My head went right through my car's windshield. I was instantly struck unconscious and rushed to a hospital where I was operated on for skull and other injuries.

"Soon after I was given the anaesthetic, I distinctly saw my body lying on the operating table. I felt myself floating out of the operating room and down a hallway in the hospital. Suddenly I felt around me the presence of departed loved ones, including my grandparents. I experienced tremendous warmth and joy. I wanted to join them right then because the feeling of love was so intense.

"But I was mentally told that I must stay in this world. My grandmother 'walked' me back to the operating room and gently and lovingly told me that someday I would join them, but not now. At that moment, I awoke and found myself conscious.

"I had never been a religious person," Andrew comments, "but the experience left me with an absolute faith in God and a greater appreciation for life and other people."

The Lady in White

Sandra is a forty-four-year-old marketing assistant in Charlotte, North Carolina. The younger of two children, she was raised as a Catholic in suburban Milwaukee. "When I was about four," Sandra recalls, "my brother developed the measles. Our family doctor gave me an inoculation so I would have a less severe case. Unfortunately, it worked in reverse and nearly proved fatal."

"As I lay in bed," Sandra remembers, "I could see the thick blankets covering the windows from my view, and I was also aware of a gentle lady in white who sat quietly next to my bed throughout my illness. Eventually I recovered.

"For years I assumed that the lady in white was a nurse. It was almost thirty years later, when my mother was talking about how I had almost died from the measles inoculation, that I mentioned the 'kindly nurse' she had hired. Only then did I learn that there had been no nurse or any other person sitting next to me during my illness. My mother and I agreed that the figure must have been my guardian angel."

Appalachian Tolling

Phillip is a sixty-six-year-old landscape architect now living in Toronto, Canada. The older of two children, he grew up in a Protestant family in New Hampshire. "I was a sickly child, and for most of my sixth year I had been ill with whooping cough, measles, and tonsillitis in rapid succession," Phillip recalls. "The culmination was a severe infection of my heart's mitral valve, known as 'rheumatic heart' in those days.

"Initially, the general practitioner/surgeon on my case was afraid to operate lest I die under the anaesthetic. My mother thereupon switched physicians. The climax came one night, and my mother and the new physician (I was later told) spent sixteen hours over me. Nevertheless, I was dying.

"All rational methods having failed, my mother then resorted to crude folk magic (although she wouldn't have called it so): loudly calling my name, over and over, until some response was elicited. In Southern Appalachian custom, this technique is known as *tolling*.

"Anyway, my sick body was certainly in the room. 'I' was elsewhere, though: 'I' was drifting like a leaf in a very gentle fall through still air—by irregular and easy swoops—in a slow, Alice-down-the-rabbit-hole motion. The relaxed, serene feeling was wonderful. I experienced a joyful acceptance of the flight or fall.

"It felt as though I were going home, or were on the threshold of home: comfortable, relaxed, and certain. I had a pervasive sense of an eventual and beneficent 'soft landing' at some destination quite a long time off. Yet the flight was in itself immensely fulfilling.

"My immediate surrounding was of a slightly slanting rain of line segments of some substance resembling a creamy-colored spaghetti, in random lengths following closely on one another along the line of travel. These formed a thick curtain of unknown but considerable depth. Beyond, I somehow knew, was a comfortable, warm darkness of infinite extent. The flight was so enjoyable, it was the greatest peace I had ever known.

"Then, ever so far off, I began to hear my mother's voice calling my name. The vision began to fade, and I knew that I had to go back. I resented the interference, the intrusion and the perceived demand, but I couldn't resist. There was no choice."

Phillip comments: "I'm not sure how this experience affected my view of life. Perhaps it predisposed me to mysticism and introspection. Certainly it contributed to my present interest in religion and metaphysics. As a wounded combat soldier on a French battlefield during World War II, I again had a near-death experience, but that's another story."

Guardian Angel at the Beach

Kelly is a thirty-year-old receptionist who has lived most of her life in southern California. The oldest of three sisters, she was nominally raised a Catholic. "We were living in Long Beach when I was five or six," Kelly recalls, "and one day we went down to the beach for a picnic. The day was unusually overcast, and I think my parents were hoping that the weather would clear up.

"When we got to the beach, it was almost completely deserted. Only a couple of people could be seen, walking, far away from our area. As we settled down on our blanket, my parents sternly warned me not to venture near the waves, which were crashing high and were much too difficult for a small child to control.

"Unfortunately, I didn't listen to them. While their attention was occupied by my two younger sisters, I quietly slipped away and ran down to the beautiful sandy beach.

"I was playing and laughing," Kelly remembers, "and I happened to look up and notice my family far away on the beach. I could plainly see our red-striped beach umbrella, but could barely make out my parents. Then I turned to the ocean.

"The waves were rolling high, and they seemed inviting to me. The air was gray-blue and slightly chilly. I thought to myself, 'No one can stop me now. I'm going into the water!'

"I actually took one step. Then a gentle but firm hand touched my right shoulder, preventing me from taking another step. I turned around, fully expecting to see my mother ready to spank me, but there was nothing. I spun around and looked behind me, in front of me, on the sand, in the water, and even in the air. Nothing. No one.

"Nevertheless, I sensed a calm presence around me. That frightened me, because I couldn't see anyone. I was so scared that I ran without stopping all the way back to my family huddled on the beach blanket. Seeing my frightened expression, my mother looked up and asked if anything was wrong. She obviously didn't know where I had come from. I simply shook my head."

Kelly remarks: "The experience changed my life. After that, I really felt watched over—and felt a connection to God and all life around me."

"Let the Waves Carry You"

Ellen is a forty-two-year-old psychotherapist and author who has lived most of her life in New York City. An only child, she was raised in a nonobservant Jewish family. "One summer's day when I was ten," Ellen recalls, "I traveled to Manhattan Beach, off the Brooklyn shore, with my best friend and her mother. It was hot and humid, and my friend and I went swimming. I happened to be a very good swimmer.

"Suddenly I got caught in the undertow. I didn't realize that I was being pushed very far out, definitely beyond where I was allowed to swim. I started swimming as hard as I could to get back to the shoreline.

"Then the waves began hitting me, and I started going under. The first time it happened, I wasn't really afraid, probably because I didn't understand what was going on. The second time it happened, I got scared as I realized that I was in real trouble and there was no one around to save me.

"I was near the rocks at that point, at least one hundred yards from the beach. I was getting more and more frightened, but I hadn't panicked yet, probably because I felt that I was such a good swimmer.

"Suddenly I went under and stayed under longer than I had before, and then I panicked. I was frantic. I felt myself thrashing with wild fear, and then suddenly I distinctly heard a voice inside me saying, 'Why don't you just relax and let the waves carry you? It's safe.'

"The voice had no age or gender. It had no connection to anything I had been taught in religious school. I felt as if—and this will sound strange—the water were talking to me, telling me what to do. Maybe it was a higher wisdom inside myself, or both of these aspects.

"In either case, I felt strongly that if I followed the advice, I would be all right. At that same moment, I forever lost my fear of death: I felt that beneath the rolling waves, which had a kind of violence to them, there was an underlying calm and gentleness.

"Well, I listened to that inner voice. What happened was

that I ended up going toward the rocks, and then someone saw me and yanked me in. My body got cut by the rocks, but I didn't even feel the pain while I was in the water."

Ellen continues, "I told a few people about my near-drowning, but I never revealed to anyone exactly what I had experienced. Somehow I felt uneasy they would judge it or try to invalidate it. I never really forgot the episode, but when I reached my midthirties, it became extremely important to me.

"I was going through a series of terribly difficult life events, including a divorce, my father's death, and my mother's subsequent illness and my having to take care of her. I felt as though I were fighting and struggling—like drowning, in a way—in the events of my life.

"That's when the message of my near-death experience became very important to me: *Let the waves carry you. It's safe.* I've used that message to guide my life in a day-to-day way: don't fight the events but flow with them, and in this way you'll find the underlying calmness."

Near-Death in the Ohio Valley

Susan is a fifty-five-year-old rehabilitation technician living in southern Florida. The fifth-born of eight children, she grew up in a small farming village in the Ohio Valley. "It was a primitive upbringing," Susan recalls, "and we had no electricity or running water until my late teens. We grew much of our own food and made our own clothes. I was reared in a hard-shell Baptist religion that had no room for deeply personal inner experiences. But I always felt an affinity for nature and loved being outdoors.

"Two weeks after my fifteenth birthday," Susan recalls, "my parents had taken me to a church revivalist meeting when my appendix suddenly burst. They hurriedly drove me to the local hospital, and then I was left alone in the emergency room with the glaring lights. Much deliberation transpired as to whether surgery was required. It was, and in the operating room it was exactly a quarter to midnight when the ether cap was placed over my nose and mouth.

"The doctors and nurses were laughing and joking about the New Year's party they had recently attended. My exact thoughts were, 'I'm lying here dying and nobody cares. All they care about is their damn party. Well, I'll just leave here and get away from them!'

"I experienced myself getting up from the operating table, striding across the room, and raising the window, through which I made my exit. As I sat on the windowsill on my way out, I turned and looked back. The doctors and nurses were continuing with their surgical procedures: preparing my body and the instruments, draping my body with sterile cloth, and still laughing and chatting about their party. I thought, 'They care so little, they don't even know I'm not there.' The light overhead glared bright.

"Then I proceeded to go out the window. At first I felt myself floating to the ground below. Then suddenly I was whisked through a dark tunnel. The sound within it resembled a billion locust wings rubbing together. Then I found myself at the edge of a beautiful meadow.

"The brilliance and colors were beyond description. A beautiful little rabbit bounded to my right, with every flower imaginable in full bloom. Instinctively I knew that the path through the meadow led to a brilliant light far greater than the brilliance lighting the meadow and surrounding forest. I also knew that the bunny would accompany me through the meadow. He was as happy and peaceful as I in this setting of splendor.

"We crossed the meadow and proceeded through the forest toward the light. I felt great, and then I wondered what my family would think or say or do, or—

"Suddenly I was in the hospital bed and screaming with pain and vomiting. A nurse jabbed me with a needle. My mother was wiping my mouth, chin, and face with a cool, damp washcloth. Dad had a hand on my head and another on my shoulder. They were telling me that the operation was over, and I would 'be okay now.' "

Susan eagerly recounted her strange, wonderful experience, but neither her family members nor teenage friends believed her. "They all just explained it away as nothing but an ether-induced dream. Eventually, I stopped telling people. I knew it was like no dream that I had ever experienced, but had been a real brush with death. Today I'm active with the Unity Church movement and have a strong interest in esoteric Christianity."

5

The Wonder of Prayer

*For the Great Spirit is everywhere; he hears whatever is in
our minds and hearts, and it is not necessary to speak to
him in a loud voice.*

——BLACK ELK

AUTHENTIC prayer has become a lost art in contemporary society. For many of us, prayer is merely a
beautiful abstraction with little personal applica-
bility. In olden times, people seem to have found it much
easier to pray, perhaps feeling more acutely a kinship with
things beyond themselves. They were closer to nature and to
one another then, and far less able to insulate themselves in
any enduring way.

To be sure, many of us experience a need to pray at times.
But we tend to feel awkward and unsure of how to do so
meaningfully. Sensing that rote habit is destructive to this
sacred endeavor, we may seek to express ourselves spontaneously. But to do this well seems no easy matter. Often, we
compromise with half-hearted praying during formal religious occasions and hope that something worthwhile has
emerged.

Is prayer a natural activity for us? The following reports
reveal that spontaneous prayer—whether an outpouring of

joy, elation, or concern—is an important feature of childhood spirituality. The act of praying intensely for others can help youngsters to overcome the trait of selfishness. It can also serve as a trigger for transcendental experience as well.

Clearly, the heavier our adult "armor" of emotional defensiveness, the less capable we are of entering the exalted world of heartfelt and healing prayer. In this regard, we have much to remember and relearn from our earliest years.

Walking with God

Peggy is a forty-two-year-old woman living in rural Minnesota. The oldest of three, she grew up in Oklahoma, where her family was active in the Church of Christ. "One fine spring day when I was six," Peggy recalls, "I was walking home from school and thinking about the minister's Sunday sermon. He had spoken about the importance of prayer and how we should talk to God every day. Since I was walking alone at that moment, I decided to begin the habit right then.

"In a sincere and happy voice, I talked aloud to God about the birds and the beautiful flowers I had seen that day. I also told God about the mean dog living up our block, and how he shouldn't make any more mean dogs or mean people.

"I interrupted my conversation with God when I suddenly spied a little horned toad crouched in a bush. I managed to catch it, and then told God how impressed I was by the way He had made the toad. I suppose I was laughing and skipping all the while. I felt so happy and contented.

"But when I got home," Peggy remembers, "my mother seemed in a very angry mood. She told me that several 'older ladies' had just been telephoning to say that I was 'talking to myself' and they were concerned for my 'mental health.' Then my mother firmly tried making me promise that I would never talk to God like this again.

"The whole episode had a tremendous effect upon me. It made me wonder why many people didn't like God and didn't want to talk with Him about everything. I became determined to keep my conversations with God as my 'personal friend,' and *not* to care particularly about others' beliefs or opinions. The experience gave me a lot of confidence and even courage, because I always felt that God was protecting me.

"Eventually I married a minister and have long since been busy with church activities, especially concerning children. I might add too that my childhood experience convinced me that if I talk things over with God and proceed, then He will provide the means—or create an event—for things to happen for my ultimate, best interest."

From Tears to Joy

Nancy is a forty-three-year-old media teacher living in rural Arkansas. She recalls: "When I was eight, my mother was diagnosed as having schizophrenia and committed to a psychiatric hospital. One of my sisters and I were sent to live with our maternal grandparents. Two younger sisters stayed with our other grandmother. When this sudden arrangement began, I felt very unhappy and lonely. I cried myself to sleep many times.

"My mother had many emotional problems," Nancy continues, "but she did teach us well to say our prayers before going to sleep. One night, as I was praying and crying for my mother, I knew that my head was 'resting in Jesus' lap.' I felt no bright light, heard no small voice. But I was filled with the knowledge that God was there and caring for me.

"It was exactly what I needed: a physical presence and a loving touch. The next morning I still felt uplifted, and for the first time had the sensation that I would be able to deal with my life's difficulties. Even now I feel tears in my eyes as I relate the experience."

Married to a minister for more than twenty years, Nancy observes: "I strongly believe that God directs his people, that there are spiritual gifts, and that there's power in prayer."

Message of the Snow

Helen is a middle-aged instructional technologist who lives in rural Michigan. The oldest of three children, she was raised in a Catholic family near Detroit. "I was about nine years old," Helen recalls, "when my mom had a serious asthma attack. She was rushed by ambulance to the hospital. My dad hastily went with her and instructed my brother and me to contact our next-door neighbor if we needed anything before he returned home.

"I was afraid for my mother's life," Helen remembers, "and decided to read the Bible. It opened onto the Gospel of John. I surprised myself in doing this, for we weren't a very religious family and we seldom even attended church. Nevertheless, I definitely felt better after reading from Scripture.

"The next day, I dressed myself and headed for the nearby church. I hadn't gone in a long time, and definitely felt inspired by the worship. As I slowly walked home from the service, I gazed at a sparkling coat of freshly fallen snow on the sidewalk beside the church. It radiated a serene beauty that seemed heavenly, as if I'd never seen snow before. Suddenly I knew that Mom, I, all of us were in good hands, and that we needn't worry about anything whatsoever. In fact, my mother did recover quickly."

Helen concludes: "I never forgot that moment of absolute certainty that there's a higher, conscious love in which we're grounded. I know that this love is enduring and of ultimate significance."

Midnight Lamentations[12]

Rabbi Dov B. Edelstein is spiritual director of Congregation Sherah Israel in Macon, Georgia. A scion of seven generations of Hasidic rabbis, he was born in a small village in Transylvania, Romania. It was the period between the two world wars, not long before the Holocaust was to erupt. "I was perhaps seven years old," Rabbi Edelstein recalls, "when one night I couldn't fall asleep. Through my bedroom window a huge moon—all full and complete—stared into my eyes. The more I looked at it, the more animated it seemed. I wanted to turn aside, yet my fascination with the moon wouldn't let me.

"Then I heard faint sounds coming from father's room. I listened in bewilderment. He was uttering words and sobbing intermittently. All shaking, I opened the door. I saw my surprised father looking up at me from the floor, where he was sitting in a corner. He gently took my hand and seated me beside him.

"It was then that I heard for the first time of Judaism's midnight lamentations, and of God's 'roaring like a lion' and the 'two boiling tears He sheds into the ocean.' That night's impressions would stay with me, ever vivid, undimmed."

Six years passed, and young Dov was studying Jewish teachings in a Hebrew academy away from home. "Sitting on the floor of my room one night, I was waiting, waiting for a sign that I had been remembered by God. I felt compelled to rise and rush into the deserted streets, to shout for my salvation, indeed, for the salvation of the whole world. Yet some power, stronger and more sublime than my desire, nailed me to the floor."

Suddenly he heard a divine voice within, lamenting over the Holy Temple's destruction. "The time had come," recollects Rabbi Edelstein. "I removed my shoes, spread ashes on my head, and chanted prayers for the ancient ceremony of the midnight vigil. I did as my father and grandfathers had done before me. I asked the Holy One, blessed be He, for deliverance."

As soon as the boy had uttered these prayers, "I felt great relief. I saw myself a partner of the Holy Presence. Surely my vigil had shortened the days of Jewish exile. Surely the days of the Messiah were near at hand."

With strong religious fervor, Dov decided to make the midnight vigil a twice-weekly event. He did so until the Nazis invaded Hungary and he was eventually sent to a concentration camp, where he was among the few to survive. Active today in Holocaust memorial and interfaith activities, the rabbi regards his youthful prayer vigils as a key feature of his spiritual life.

Awakening to God

Millie is a sixty-eight-year-old woman living in Toledo, Ohio. She recalls: "At the age of ten I abruptly awakened one night from a sound sleep. It's very hard to put into words, but somehow I acutely felt the presence of God.

"I cried and cried, and kept repeating, 'God, please don't let me waste my life!'

"Eventually," Millie remembers, "I fell asleep with a feeling of great peace and inner certainty. That episode has stayed with me for more than fifty-five years."

God, My Friend

"Ours was not a happy family, though we tried to pretend it was. My father was an abusive alcoholic, and my mother suffered from schizophrenia," recalls Carmine. A forty-three-year-old special educator living in Maryland, she is the oldest of three children. "I attended Catholic school, but the emphasis on rituals and beliefs just didn't feel right to me.

"One spring day, when I was thirteen," Carmine recollects, "I sat down next to the large bush in my backyard and pondered what I had been told about God. I tried to understand why, if God had intended me for a contemplative, He/She had placed me in such a constantly noisy household, and why I had begun to menstruate.

"I sat to consider all this for what seemed to be five or ten minutes. I still cannot explain what happened, except that I felt in touch with something immensely real and comforting. When I stood up, I understood that God cared for me and was my friend—and that while I might sometimes *feel* alone, I would never truly *be* alone.

"I went back inside my house. To my astonishment, my family demanded to know where I had been for the past two hours!"

Today Carmine is active with the Quakers. "The experience helped reassure me," she comments, "that there is more to life than the adults around me were teaching."

Praying for Mother's Life

Charles is a seventy-three-year-old man living in Tucson, Arizona. Raised in a rural environment, he is currently writing a book about Martin Luther's teachings. "Largely because of my mother's concern for her children, my life journey began with prayer. My earliest experience of private prayer happened when I was four or five years old. With a couple of my sisters, I slept in the same bedroom with our parents.

"One night I suddenly awoke to my mother's heavy, labored breathing. I became frightened and began thinking, 'What if she's going to die?'

"I lay awake tossing and couldn't fall asleep for many hours. Then suddenly I had the thought to ask God to let mother live until I was twenty-one. To me, it seemed like an almost unimaginably long way off. Convinced that my utterly sincere prayer had been answered, I soon fell asleep.

"The years passed," continues Charles, "and exactly one week before my twenty-second birthday, my mother died. It was not until we returned home from the cemetery that I remembered my long-ago prayer as a preschool child.

"When I related this account to a friend recently, he asked me, 'What if you had asked God to let your mother live until you were fifty?' I had indeed pondered this question many times. My answer to him was this: 'God certainly knew when she would leave this life. So He gave me that particular prayer, so that when she died I would remember and thank Him for answering my prayer.' "

Charles recollects another vivid encounter with prayer: "When I was about thirteen years old, one of my sisters became seriously ill with a severe case of spinal meningitis. After the doctor's visit to our home, father called all of us children together. He recounted the doctor's worried report and then asked us to pray for our sister. I went into my bedroom and, for the first time in my life, knelt in prayer. I simply asked God to make my sister well.

"When I rose from my knees," Charles comments, "I *knew* she would get well. I went into the barn where my two older sisters were doing their chores and fighting back their tears. I tried to comfort them with the assurance I had received from God. Sure enough, my sister recovered without any after-effects. The nurses called it a miracle!"

"The Body of Christ"

Martha, the high school English teacher whom we met in chapter 3, also relates the following episode: "One day when I was six or seven, I was being compelled to take a nap. I was lying on my bed and gazing out the upstairs window. After a few minutes I began indulging in a free-floating reverie, as I often did. This time, perhaps because of my recent religious instruction, I started thinking about the Body of Christ.

"What followed then," Martha recalls vividly, "was a sudden influx of insight that all the world—our earth, trees, houses, people, sky, birds, and clouds—all existed within the Body of Christ. I envisioned this enormous, pervasive God floating in eternal space and containing all of the 'world' within Him. Then I felt myself existing as an infinitesimally small but vital part of this great Body. This awareness was all-consuming.

"With a wonderful and joyous feeling, I ran downstairs to tell my mother. To my shock, she was distressed by what I had recounted and insisted that I put it out of my mind at once. Though I loved my mother, I decided to reject her advice and have always remembered the experience."

No longer active in the Catholic church, Martha comments: "I don't think I was singled out or specially 'chosen.' Since I was schooled in Catholicism, my inner self as a child found expression in that religion's images."

Longing to Pray

Carol is the forty-five-year-old former president of her synagogue in her hometown, Chicago. The younger of two children, she grew up in a fairly observant Jewish home. But because she was a girl, her parents were hesitant to provide formal religious training, such as learning to read Hebrew. "This frustrated me a great deal," Carol recalls, "and by the time I was nine, I longed to say prayers at bedtime. I envied the child in the famous Norman Rockwell painting with her hands clasped and kneeling by her bedside. I wanted a 'bedtime-anytime' prayer.

"My need for prayer was a secret. I told no one. Then, one evening, I looked in my father's Friday night prayerbook. It had a black cover, and was small and well worn, filled with Hebrew and English words. It was the only religious book in our house, and it had always conveyed to me a sense that from it, one could say 'Jewish' words to God.

"Without being observed—due to my fear of embarrassment—I quietly searched through its thin, translucent pages. Suddenly the book fell open onto a page arranged differently from the others. There were more empty spaces, fewer words, shorter sentences, and larger type. It was as though this page was waiting for me and presenting something my size. The prayer was just right. I said it and was full:

Hear O Israel
the Lord our God
the Lord is one.

"This childhood experience was probably my first effort to reach for something that I could call my own, in my limited Jewish life," Carol comments. "It represented my small voice calling out for divine guidance, for I believe I've always been searching for the answers that feel right to me. Though the episode occurred many years ago, it has led directly to my involvement with Judaism today."

South Dakota Tornado

A single parent, Christine is a thirty-six-year-old graduate student attending the University of Hawaii. With two sisters, she grew up in a Lutheran family on the edge of a small South Dakota town. "One Sunday afternoon when I was about seven years old," Christine recalls, "all five of us were outside chatting and playing when the first signs of a tornado started to appear.

"Though it was still sunny, there appeared dark, boiling clouds nearby. The chirping birds were suddenly hushed. My father and two sisters went inside, but against my mother's urgings, I remained in front of the house. Mother and our neighbor Sally (who wore crutches) scanned the skies for a pale V shape that indicated a tornado.

"Suddenly my mother cried out, 'There it is!' I can still see everyone as they were at that instant—our neighbor Sally near her garage, my mother standing on the slope between the houses, my father holding my younger sister in his arms, and my older sister beside him, before the picture window inside the house.

"Very frightened, I felt certain the tornado was going to land close and that neither Sally nor my mother nor I would reach the basement in time. I was sure that the wind's force would shatter the window behind which my father and older sister stood.

"I turned my back to the tornado and faced our garage door. I began praying to God to spare us all. I felt my prayer reaching a very, very deep level within, and then suddenly I knew with complete confidence that the tornado wouldn't affect us. When I turned back toward the tornado, it was gone. I *knew* that my prayer to God had somehow been connected with the tornado's vanishing. When I think back and put myself into that long-ago moment, I again have no doubt.

"Today I'm a practicing Quaker," Christine concludes, "and I look back on this incident as a special gift to me. I've always tended to intellectualize and mentally dissect events in my life, but this one refuses such attempts."

The Answer of the Trees

Jonathan is a thirty-year professional singer who has spent most of his life in the New York City area. The middle of three brothers, he grew up in an observant Jewish home. "It was my fourteenth summer," he recalls, "and I was staying at an overnight camp in the Catskill Mountains. Early adolescence was proving to be a difficult time for me, and away from my parents and neighborhood friends, I had run out of answers for my life.

"One morning I woke very early and felt that I needed to be

alone. As I walked to the nearby woods, I inwardly asked for guidance from above. I took along my prayerbook, found a quiet, leafy spot, and began to utter the Hebrew words aloud to God. Suddenly the woods began to rumble. All the trees around me began to sway, as though there were a sudden storm. As soon as I became aware of this situation and looked around, everything stopped just as abruptly."

Jonathan remembers: "It was all so strange. This time, I specifically asked God to show me His presence as a clear sign. The instant I returned to reciting my prayers aloud from the prayerbook, the rumbling and swaying resumed, then immediately subsided."

"I truly felt that a spiritual confirmation—an answer about God's presence in my life—had come to me, and that I was being listened to. I left the woods with new confidence and a sense of purpose.

"But the experience wasn't just fleeting," Jonathan emphasizes. "It made a profound impression on me. I became convinced that prayer is real and important, just as the Bible teaches. That summer I spent at overnight camp became a turning point in my life toward spiritual things, and toward my approach to communicating with God on a regular basis."

Beyond the Stars

Janice is a fifty-year-old registered nurse living in rural Indiana. The oldest child of a Baptist minister, Janice grew up near Nashville, Tennessee. "My Baptist grandparents were my spiritual role models. When I was very young, I heard them say that I should 'pray without ceasing,' and I tried very hard to do just that. After several years it seems that I learned to pray with great intensity, even when I wasn't forming words of formal prayer. Eventually, in my prayers, I began occasionally to feel a 'presence' move through me, which filled me with wonder and awe. I felt hungrier for further 'visitations.'

Janice remembers: "I was ten when my first vivid experience occurred. I had already discovered that at nighttime I could best maintain this inward state. I would kneel on the bed with my elbows on the windowsill above it and pray for hours before finally lying down to sleep.

"One night, as I gazed through my window at the starry night, I thought how God was *through*, and yet *beyond*, all space. Suddenly I had the sensation of being surrounded by a musical harmony like a great anthem, only inaudible to the human ear. Then I just seemed to evaporate until I too was *through* and *beyond* the stars."

"I was completely filling space, and the musical harmony was completely filling me. I did not see the proverbial Light, I experienced it. I did not hear the anthem, I *was* it. There was no sense of time, so I have no idea how long it was until I suddenly felt I had journeyed too far. Grabbing the window frame and curtains, I forcefully returned to my bed. I didn't feel as though merely my soul or spirit had traveled, I felt as if my entire being—including my body—had made the journey, and yet I knew I had physically never left my bed."

Janice also recounts: "When I was fifteen, I had another mystical experience involving prayer. One night I was thinking about the Bible as I knelt to pray. The words that occupied my mind were those heard by Moses at the burning bush: 'I am that I am.' Suddenly I felt myself hurled into star-filled space, return to my room and innermost being, and then hurtle back into the stars. Then I understood that 'I am that I am' also described my own identity: that the innermost *me* was also the utmost divinity. It was all me. It was all God. Everything in the universe was one."

6

Simple Moments of Ecstasy

This cornucopia of air! This very heaven of simple day!
—CONRAD AIKEN

WHEN was the last time you experienced intense delight or joy while performing a commonplace act of daily living? If you resemble most active adults in our society, then the answer almost certainly is: not very recently.

Yet, the world's great religions have for centuries taught that a holiness is present in all moments of human life. Although this notion has been expressed in myriad ways, the underlying message has remained remarkably constant: that every instant of human existence, no matter how seemingly simple, is a portal to bliss.

For many of us, this teaching is comforting and even inspiring. In practical terms, though, it often remains an elusive ideal. The plain fact is that we seldom experience unalloyed pleasure—let alone ecstasy—in the ordinary aspects of life. Indeed, we tend to generate almost impossibly high expectations for getaway trips and the like, precisely because we find everyday routine to be dull and lacking in truly fulfilling moments.

Is this situation changeable? Is there a way of bridging the world of timeless spiritual truth with the actuality of our calendar pace?

The following accounts would definitely suggest so. While varying tremendously in their specific content, they are united in demonstrating that, at least during childhood, we can achieve exalted states of consciousness by virtue of absolutely casual events: listening to music in a moment of reverie, taking a walk on a spring afternoon, or watching the dancing of dust motes in kitchen sunlight.

Rural Highway Ecstasy

Renée is a forty-three-year-old commercial artist living in Los Angeles. The younger of two children, she grew up Catholic in northern California. "I was five when I had an experience that changed my whole view of life. Putting it into words is by far the most difficult thing possible for me.

"My parents, my sister, and I were riding along the rural highway near Lodi," recalls Renée. "My sister and I were sitting quietly in the back seat, and the sun was shining into the car. In a quiet reverie, I was looking at my arm, which was poised across my legs.

"I looked up and out the car window. Suddenly, *as if a slide had changed in a theater*, the scenery somehow became different. I can't accurately say that time stood still—time just simply wasn't. Everything looked the same as it had a moment before, yet it was more so.

"I felt instantly at home in the universe, and *knew*—I can't emphasize this enough—God's essence. I became the trees that I saw, the birds, the blades of grass, the sky, the hills, even the car.

"Everything was everything. It was the total cosmos, and all of it was me. And so, viewing this in all its unfettered simplicity, I was able to see how All was connected—not like pieces in a puzzle, but how everything was absolutely necessary to the whole, or none of it could be at all.

"I turned my head back to the car's inside, and my eyes met my arm still draped over my legs. I remember distinctly, as I felt myself flying back to this reality, saying to myself: 'My God, I'm trapped inside this body. I'm a soul, trapped in this body, and I can't get out! Then I knew that my soul could never die. It was the part of me that was God, and I immediately wanted to find my way back to oneness again."

Renée observes: "After this experience, I longed to go to church every Sunday. I became very religious and wanted to learn all I could about God. Institutional religion was very unsatisfying to me, though. It was in the late 1960s, when I first began reading about Taoism and Zen, that I reencountered the God of my childhood vision of oneness and wholeness."

British Wall and Sky

Rowena is a seventy-year-old retired teacher who has lived her whole life in England. An only child, she grew up in a nominally Methodist family in Warwickshire County. "I think I was about ten," Rowena recalls, "when one sunny day in autumn I was coming through a dark passageway between two old houses in my town. Holding on to the gate's latch, I was suddenly brought to a stop by the sight of the house's warm, old brick wall jutting against the blue of the sky.

"For some reason I immediately thought of God—being out there, up there, in the dazzling blue sky. In the very next instant I was overwhelmed by the awareness that God was also in the bricks, and everywhere—in everything that I saw, everything that I sensed, and everything that I touched. I felt that God surrounded me, and though I surely couldn't have verbalized it at the time in these words, I knew that God was good, He was love.

"It was such a relief," Rowena remarks. "The experience solved many problems for me. Since then I've gone through many ups and downs about faith and organized religion. But there's always been this unshakable truth holding me up and reassuring me. Always, my vivid memory of the brick wall against the blue sky, my hand on the gate's latch—and my great flood of joy at the sudden understanding that was given to me—comes warmly in and steadies me."

First-Grade Oneness

Alex is a forty-four-year-old electrical engineer living in northern California. He recalls: "One fine, sunny day during first grade, I was suddenly overcome by the feeling that the secrets of life were mine. The experience lasted about thirty seconds, but is still unforgettable. I was standing near my desk with some classmates when this occurred, and I mentioned the experience as it was occurring, but they all just stared at me blankly.

"I don't remember having any particular religious or spiritual outlook at that age," comments Alex. "My main interest was in drawing and painting. Now that I'm older and have studied shamanism, among other subjects, I realize that my life has been aimed in a direction that our technological, profit-oriented society could not allow or encourage.

"So, at this late date, I pick up the threads again and make the best of it. My search has embraced yoga, Hinduism, Kabbalah, and especially Tibetan Buddhism. I've definitely been seeking to reconnect with that all-comprehending and all-encompassing childhood vision of perfection itself."

Creating Euphoria

Pierre is a sixty-year-old clinical psychologist and former professor living in Atlanta. The second-youngest of four brothers, he grew up Catholic in Normandy, France. "Very often when I was about three," Pierre recalls, "I used to look out the window of either the bathroom or the ironing room and experience a euphoric unification with the space in front of me and all around.

"I became so absorbed in these experiences that I would lose all sense of time. I would usually return, with a jolt and sadness, to the realm of the everyday things I was expected to do, concerned about whether I had been 'away' long enough to get fussed at by my governess or mother.

"Also, I distinctly remember how every afternoon until I was nine or ten I had to nap for about an hour. Often I didn't sleep; rather, I daydreamed. At some point I discovered that if I sat very still in my bed with my legs crossed and then fixed my eyes on a spot in the design of the Oriental rug, I entered a euphoric state. I had been taught prayers, but never experienced the same intensity of feeling with them."

Pierre comments: "In simple terms, these meditative experiences led me to feel as a child that the grown-ups around me were out of touch with something and were deceiving themselves—and me—with unfounded opinions. As a result,

I often felt the need to retreat to a private reality among the woods and in nature."

Playing on the Kitchen Floor

Paul is a forty-five-year-old artist living in Columbus, Ohio. The younger of two brothers, he grew up in Cleveland in a Jewish family. "I was about three," Paul recalls, when "one morning, as usual, I was sitting and playing on the linoleum kitchen floor as my mother was washing dishes in the nearby sink. It must have been spring or early summer, for the window was open and sunlight was pouring in.

"My mother was happily singing 'You are my sunshine, my only sunshine' to me as she washed the dishes. I sat looking at the sunshine and gazing at the tiny dust motes dancing in the light.

"I felt a wave of utter peace and happiness. My life was completely full at that moment. It was an ecstatic experience of complete oneness, though of course, as a child I couldn't articulate that description."

Paul comments: "I've thought of the moment often in my life, especially when I became a parent, and even more so since my mother died last year."

The Loose Tooth

Bob is a seventy-year-old retired naval officer and high school mathematics teacher now living in southern Florida. The older of two children, Bob was raised a Catholic in a New Jersey industrial town.

"One spring day when I was about seven," he recalls, "I was walking home from school as usual. It was a pleasantly sunny and comfortably warm afternoon. I was shaking a loose 'baby' tooth with my tongue, when for the first time I tasted my own blood. Nothing special happened. The next afternoon I was shaking the loose tooth with my tongue again, but when I tasted the blood, a wonderful and profound feeling came over me.

"For the first time in my young life I *knew* that I had my own, individual existence—that I was unique and different from everyone else in the world. The feeling was truly awesome, and though lasting only ten or fifteen minutes, it remains vivid to this day.

"For years after, I thought that I had been almost retarded in developing the idea of the individual self. But a few years ago, when I told a family gathering about my youthful episode involving the loose tooth, no one else at the gathering had undergone such an intense identity experience.

"I can recall almost everything since my first day of school at age five," adds Bob. "At age fifty I prepared a photo album of family members as a wedding gift when our first child was getting married.

"The 'I' within me recalled every picture of me from a five-year-old through my teens, then college years, young parenthood, and middle age. But the striking thing about preparing the photo album was the awareness it catalyzed: My body had changed tremendously, but the 'I' was the same. For the first time in my life, I truly understood my childhood experience: that the 'I' (my real self) is not only unique but also changeless.

"You might think, because of my major health problems," Bob concludes, "that it's a sad time for my wife and me. But on the contrary, it's one of the happiest, most enriching periods of our lives. I eagerly look forward to the next world, after I drop this three-dimensional body."

Bench in the Sun

Pierre, the French-born psychologist quoted earlier in this chapter, relates: "When I was about seven or eight, my friend Jacques, who lived in a château some five miles away, came to spend the day with me. After several enjoyable hours, my governess, my younger brother, and I accompanied Jacques back to the railroad station.

"It was a sunny summer afternoon, and we all sat on a bench waiting for the train. We were facing west and had the sun in our faces. It was pleasantly warm.

"All of a sudden I became euphoric sitting there. The others continued their quiet conversation, but I couldn't or wouldn't pull myself away from this absorption in the light and peace and the sense of spaciousness that surrounded me. I experienced the awareness that everything was fully what it was, all the time: there was nothing lacking, no tension, and no 'else.'

"It was a profoundly peaceful few minutes," Pierre remembers, "and the memory has intensified in recent years because of my meditative practice. I was fussed at a lot by my governess and other adults in the household, and the episode gave me an important glimpse of another way of being."

The Face in the Window

Sandra Rouja is a professional writer living in Bermuda, where she was born and raised. "Sometime during my eleventh year," Sandra recalls, "I was on the morning school bus as usual. It was crowded that particular morning, meaning that I had to stand all the way. As usual, I wasn't quite ready for class, having fallen asleep over my books the night before. At best, my young life was very confusing, with my recently divorced mother and the austere grandmother with whom we lived—and school, where the classes did not give me answers to what I wanted so desperately to know, and where I felt like a strange outsider.

"That morning, as the bus sped on its way, my mind was absorbed by all of these things. Just before the bus began to slow down for the school stop, it passed a small wooded area, which I glimpsed in a blurry haze of leafy shades of green."

Sandra reflects: "Now, forty years later, I try to measure the time frame for my passing those woods: three seconds. Within those fleeting moments, a window opened into the green haze and I saw the dark silhouette of a man's face set against a small, somber room. In my mind's eye I can still see that darkly framed room with its unknown occupant.

"But much more than what I saw was what I felt. As with one's nocturnal dreams, I cannot even begin to measure that duration.

"As though emanating from the figure in the room, a great sense of loneliness, pain, and sadness overtook me. Strangely, I felt no fear or confusion: only an intense feeling of compassion and love surrounding me, emanating from me to the stranger, and filling me with strength, understanding, power, and humility.

"The window within the green haze opened up a world of love, sadness, and wonder far beyond anything I had ever experienced as a child," Sandra observes. "I didn't feel that the man was interested or even aware of me, but rather that in some wondrous way I had been able to connect with his reality. Most important, I felt that I could affect it positively.

"As strange new thoughts of peace, love, and healing flowed through me out to the image and to the world beyond, I experienced a whole new perception of myself and everything. How this perception would fit into my life I didn't know, but I would never be the same.

"The bus jerked to a halt," Sandra remembers, "pulling me back to the immediate. Sometime during the day, I tried sharing the event with a classmate whom I hoped was my friend. How was I to know that my experience wasn't part of other children's reality? If I had felt 'different' before, I was now 'known' to be odd. It would be almost twenty years before I could—or would—share the experience with anyone else. Nevertheless, it dramatically changed my perception of myself and prepared me for a lifetime of inner awakenings and acceptances."

Fourth-Grade Visions of Unity

Andrea is a twenty-nine-year-old radio disc jockey living in Vermont. She recalls: "When I was in fourth grade, I would have days that were incomprehensible to my child's mind. It's very hard to put into words. I would feel a tremendous connectedness to everything and everyone. Everything was one. I could see the connection between all things. Of course, at the time I had no idea what was going on.

"I would try to convey my experience to friends and family," remembers Andrea, "but no one paid much attention. Some days I wasn't able to communicate with people at all because my perceptions of unity were too overwhelming. This was interpreted by others as extreme shyness.

"Actually, I wasn't the slightest bit shy. I was just grateful at not being locked away, because I was convinced that

something was very wrong with me. These intense perceptions lasted for more than a year, and then gradually faded
away.

"Much later, in college, I tried mescaline and was amazed
to find myself feeling the same things I had felt as a fourth-
grader: an all-consuming love for everything and everyone.
It's only been recently that I've truly begun to understand the
deep spirituality of my childhood experiences."

Little League Bliss

Jerry is a forty-seven-year-old clinical psychologist and professor living in Chicago. He recalls: "When I was about
eleven, I participated in Little League baseball. Unfortunately,
I wasn't a very well coordinated hitter. One afternoon we
were having an important game against the top team in the
league. It was the bottom of the last inning, and we were one
run behind. There were two men on base, two outs, and it was
nearly my turn to bat.

"I wasn't yet in my religious phase," Jerry continues, "but I
had prayed vigorously in the on-deck circle for the batter
ahead of me to resolve the issue. But he walked, and now the
bases were loaded. As I stepped to the batter's box, I softly
prayed, 'Oh God, please don't let me embarrass myself!' with
more intensity than I had thought possible.

"I let the first pitch go by. Strike one. On the next pitch,
something happened. As the pitcher began his regular
windup, the illumination on the field seemed to become
brighter, and everything became silent and luminous. Everything went into slow motion. I found myself observing—
hearing—thinking—with absolute clarity and calm that I was

going to slam the ball into right field, and everything would be all right.

"The pitch came, and the ball floated in as big as a basketball. I hit it squarely and it flew just over the second baseman's mitt into right field.

"The world went into real time and color. I ran to first, tumbled onto the grass, and laughed until I cried. The runners scored and the game was over."

Jerry relates: "I never talked to anyone about the incident until many years later. By then, I had undergone other experiences that led me to explore parapsychology. However, I did become a great believer in prayer, and I still am."

"Somewhere over the Rainbow"

Steven is a forty-year-old psychologist living in a suburb of New York City. The older of two sons, he grew up in a close, middle-class Jewish family. "My mother taught music," he recalls, "and sometimes at home she would play the piano and sing aloud. When I was about seven or eight, she would often play the song 'Somewhere over the Rainbow' from the movie version of *The Wizard of Oz*.

"On occasion, when I sat playing with toys on the floor nearby," Steven recollects, "this particular song would induce a trancelike state of reverie. It would depend on my state of mind, I guess, because it didn't happen all the time. But sometimes I felt like the music and the images of the words were taking me far, far away from my reality of being a little boy playing on the floor.

"There was a yearning quality in the music that somehow touched me deeply. At the same time, I would feel that part of me was already somewhere high above the heavens, 'over the rainbow,' just like the song was saying.

"The sensation that accompanied this awareness was one of complete euphoria—as though I were back in a wonderfully familiar place that I had somehow forgotten in my task of being a growing boy. I felt transported to a timeless place, with sunlight in the sky and a tremendous joy inside of me.

"Today music remains one of the most important spiritual forces in my life. I'm inspired in various ways by many different kinds of music. I can't imagine living on a day-to-day basis without its beauty and power."

My Spiritual Father

Ruth is a sixty-eight-year-old retired dietitian living in New York City. "An only child, I grew up in Minneapolis during the Great Depression, and I was very poor and shy," Ruth recalls. "My parents were always quarreling, and my mother was chronically ill with ulcerative colitis. I didn't get much joy from them.

"I must have been no older than five when one day my mother announced, 'We're going to visit Zayde [Yiddish for "Grandpa"].' I sat on his lap and studied him: his yarmulke, his white beard, and especially his deep blue-green eyes. Zayde knew no English, and I knew no Yiddish then, so there were no words between us. But his eyes were full of tenderness, kindness, and empathy.

"Suddenly I experienced a glow, or flash, that permeated my entire being. This all-encompassing feeling was that my grandpa was Jewish, I was Jewish, and it was *good* to be Jewish. The emotionality of the episode was overwhelming and affected my view of life. It stays with me to this day.

"To me," Ruth comments, "Grandpa was a kind of deity, although not one to whom you prayed or feared. He was like a spiritual father to me. I never received any material gifts from him, nor did I expect any. Yet the feeling of piety that he imparted to me has lasted all my life. I never became a strictly observant Jew, but his influence led me to study Hebrew, become involved with Jewish organizations, and later, to visit Israel.

"I've heard it said that 'religious feeling has to be caught, and that it can't be taught,' " Ruth observes. "If so, then I certainly caught a deep feeling of Jewish consciousness in that one childhood episode with Grandpa."

Car Radio Reverie

Paul, the Ohio artist whom we met earlier in this chapter, recalls: "One ordinary evening when I was about nine, my parents and I had been riding around the neighborhood to do some errands. We stopped at a red light. My father ran into a store to buy cigarettes, and he left the motor running. The car radio was on, and the song was Tennessee Ernie Ford singing 'Sixteen Tons.'

"I felt relaxed while listening to it. I heard the lyrics: 'Sixteen tons and what do you get? / Another day older and deeper in debt. / Saint Peter, don't you call me, for I can't go. / I owe my soul to the company store.'

"I sat trying to figure out what these mysterious words meant, and I turned them over in my mind again and again. Suddenly all become ONE. I felt like I had fallen into an endless NOW. It was a total unitive experience of bliss, which lasted the whole length of the song and a few minutes afterward."

Paul comments: "The experience pushed me deeper into life

and made my life more intense. In particular, the song's lyrics gave me a greater sensitivity to working people. I began to see my parents in a new light, for we weren't affluent."

Making Mud Castles

Cynthia is a forty-year-old public relations specialist living in suburban New Jersey. An only child, she grew up in New York City. "I was no more than six," Cynthia recalls, "when one day I was playing on the beach on the Rockaway shore. My family had gone there for the summer. It was late afternoon, and I was alone, making mud castles ('dribbles,' as I used to call them).

"As I sat on the sandy beach, I felt a sense of joyousness beyond anything I had ever experienced. In a way, my whole life has been a spiritual search to find a way back to that glorious moment. Several years ago I realized that it possessed the three things I've always cherished most: freedom, privacy, and independence."

Walking Home from School

Herb is a seventy-six-year-old retired governmental meteorologist. Growing up in a Los Angeles suburb, he was the younger of two brothers. Herb's father had little interest in religious matters, but his mother was an ardent "New Thought" Christian who also studied Eastern philosophy.

"One spring afternoon, when I was about ten," Herb recalls, "I was walking home from school alone. Suddenly I experienced an unsurpassed feeling of happiness and understanding. Everything seemed to fall into place and possess the greatest significance. Although I still saw the same, usual surroundings, they were now unbelievably vivid. I stared entranced at my feet and the fuzzy little yellow flowers that the acacia trees had dropped on the sidewalk.

"There was no outward change in my behavior, but I wanted intensely to be alone and undisturbed, so I could experience my sudden new feeling to the fullest. I walked on home, and of course, the insight began to dim—although it lasted perhaps several hours with diminishing intensity.

"While the experience didn't keep me from being an 'ordinary' person in later life," wryly comments Herb, "it left me with a deep conviction that there is more to our existence than the brain's electrochemical activity. I haven't read Abraham Maslow in years, but I know he discussed such peak experiences, as did other thinkers before him. The episode remains so vivid for me that sixty-odd years later, it's still clear in my mind."

7

Profound Musings

How can it be that a stone, a plant, a star, can take on the burden of being?

—JAMES AGEE

F O R many decades in American society, the mass media have helped to perpetuate a popular stereotype of children as inherently empty-headed and selfish, endlessly bickering over possession of toys or scheming how to outwit their parents and teachers. Mainstream psychology, ever since its origin in the late nineteenth century, has similarly portrayed the early years as a time of utterly simplistic thinking and trivial pursuits. Almost never are we presented with an alternative, more complete, view of childhood.

For this reason the reminiscences that follow are quite important. Though varying widely in content, they clearly indicate that some, perhaps many, children engage in deep speculation about human life and death, self-awareness and transcendence, and the cosmos. Noteworthy is the frequency with which such intense and youthful contemplation seems to induce the experience of bliss.

In our hurried and high-pressured society, most of us would undoubtedly benefit from focusing our thoughts more whole-heartedly on such lofty and potentially dazzling matters.

"My Child Died in a Fire"

Paula and her husband live in rural Oklahoma. They do not have any formal religious affiliation. "We have two children," Paula relates, "and the younger is named Jennifer. She's an active thirteen-year-old with a keen interest in boys and horses. She especially loves competing at horse shows. All this is outwardly very normal, of course. But at the age of about four, Jennifer began describing several imaginary playmates at our home. She spoke of them often, and they were frequently a part of her household play, with names like 'Squirmy Worm,' 'Hawka,' 'Seepy,' 'Invisible Baby Monster,' and 'My Little Girl.'

"One afternoon Jennifer was riding with me in the car. We were having a lively and playful conversation about little girls. After a long pause, Jennifer continued speaking. But her voice became so solemn and in such contrast to the playful giggling of the previous moment that I turned my eyes from the road to look at her.

"Tears began rolling down Jennifer's face as she softly said, 'I used to have a little girl, but she died in a fire.' Then she quickly wiped her eyes and asked about something that seemed totally unrelated. Her strange and intense sadness vanished without a trace.

"Interestingly," Paula comments, "although Jennifer continued to amuse herself with imaginary playmates for another year, she never again spoke of 'My Little Girl.' I'm not well versed in this area of experience, but I've never been able to dismiss that grief-filled moment as part of her imagination. The depth of the sadness was too great. I've sometimes wondered if, by retelling the tragedy, she was letting go of something deeply painful in her past: allowing it to slip from her consciousness forever—in this lifetime, at least.

"Jennifer is now thirteen," concludes her mother, "and remembers many imaginary playmates and the names she created for them. Yet she has no memory of 'My Little Girl' or her reference to a deceased child."

Juice-Time Philosophy

Alice is an attorney living in Milwaukee. She relates that her younger son, Jeremy, is "a typical, active, outgoing four-year-old boy. I never thought he showed much tendency toward introspection. My husband and I aren't religiously affiliated, and we come from nonreligious Protestant homes. As a result, we've never discussed religious ideas with either Jeremy or his sister Karla.

"Recently I took Jeremy to the science museum. We were sitting in the cafeteria and having juice together when the following conversation ensued:

"MOTHER: I'm so proud of you! You're getting so big! Last year, when I brought you to the museum, we had to use your stroller because you were so tired and complained that you couldn't walk.

"JEREMY: Yes, but when I'm a baby again, I'm going to need my stroller.

"MOTHER: But you're getting bigger and bigger! Someday you'll be a grown man.

"JEREMY: I mean, after I'm a man, then I'm going to be a baby again . . . (*pause*). You know, after you die, you wake up!"

Alice comments: "In conversations since that day, I've never discovered any specific memories that Jeremy has about past lives. Rather, he seems to carry with him a generalized but firm impression about the reality of reincarnation. In every other way, Jeremy's interests and activities seem wholly ordinary for his age."

Talking with God

Linda is a forty-eight-year-old mother of two children living in Stamford, Connecticut. "At age three my oldest child, Kevin, had what could probably be called a peak experience. From time to time before then, he would often ask me questions about God. I don't remember exactly what he asked, but we did have an ongoing conversation about God for quite a while.

"One day Kevin was standing very pensively by the big window in our living room. He stood very still for a long time—which is amazing for an active three-year-old boy—just staring and not moving. When Kevin finally walked away from the spot, I asked what he had been doing. Very matter of factly he replied, 'I was talking with God.'

"I gently tried probing for details, but to no avail. Kevin didn't want to share them with me. He remained quite subdued for about an hour after that, and then went on playing as usual. I asked Kevin about the incident at a later point in his life, and he apparently didn't recall it."

Who Is This "I"?

Sarah is a forty-five-year-old editor at a publishing company devoted to spiritual and psychological topics. The youngest of three children, she grew up in Manhattan in an ethnically Jewish household.

One day when Sarah was about nine, she was lying on her bed and thinking. "I was trying to imagine what it would be like to be dead. I started by trying to imagine a world in which I didn't exist, but then I realized that that didn't make sense—for if I'm not in the world, then who is there to imagine it without me? I guess it was that particular thought that made me understand that the feeling of 'I' was somehow the essence of my identity.

"Next, I thought about the fact that everyone uses the word 'I' to refer to himself or herself: that everyone has this same experience of 'I.' Finally, I concluded that as long as there is anyone experiencing the existence of 'I' in the world, then *I* can never die.

"What's remarkable about this experience—though it wasn't exactly an altered state of consciousness—was its clarity and my complete sense of enlightened conviction."

"We Lived Before in Germany"

Janet is a middle-aged woman living in rural Massachusetts. She recalls: "Several years ago my oldest son, Nevin, was dying of a brain tumor. He was nine years old and receiving services in a hospice program. The counselor had determined that the time had come to discuss the topic of death with his seven-year-old brother.

"She asked what 'death' meant to him. He lay down on his brother's hospital bed, which we had in our home, and closed his eyes. He quietly said, 'I know that Nevin is going to die, but I also know that we were together before. We lived in

Germany. I was a prince and he was my brother even then. I know that we'll be together again.'

"I was shocked," recollects Janet, "because I had never mentioned reincarnation to them at all. I hadn't even been aware that he had ever heard of Germany. When I later questioned him, he had no idea where Germany was, or where he had heard of it. Interestingly, the hospice counselor related that many children have remembrances of past lives, but feel embarrassed about discussing them."

Linking to God and Infinity

Jenny is a thirty-one-year-old publisher in the New England area. Widowed several years ago, she is the middle child of five and has a young daughter. "My childhood upbringing in New Jersey was very Catholic," Jenny recollects. "I attended Catholic school, observed feast days in the home, and generally felt very religious. I aspired to become a 'devout' person and nearly every day thought about God, devotion, prayer, heaven and hell. The church's mysticism especially appealed to me. Therefore it was natural for me to use mystical principles to achieve a state of altered reality—though I didn't call it that at the time.

"The mystical experiences I now recall always involved getting myself into a 'state'—which I consciously achieved—where I would think about infinity, and then actually *be* infinite. I remember 'working myself up' in my mind—to where I could connect intensely to the thought that my sense of 'I' would never end: because I had been born just this once, 'I' would continue to exist forever.

"I would imagine—I would see—I would experience—going on and on—and never ending, or stopping, or dying. I would imagine myself and my place in the infinite—perhaps it was God's plan—and I would feel special that God had given me the opportunity to become part of that infinity.

"After I achieved that state of mind, I would feel good, and strong, and like I had accomplished something I was supposed to do. I never felt pressured by myself or anyone else to experience this inner state, but I always felt renewed after I did."

Jenny recently published a series of articles on the recovery movement and the twelve-step program, which triggered for her long-suppressed memories of both abusive and transcendent episodes during her childhood years. "I'm very interested in personal growth and spiritual discovery," Jenny comments, "and my life focus is on becoming aware and awake at all levels."

Colorado Mortuary

Stan is a forty-one-year-old man living in Colorado Springs. "My family had a mortuary in a small town in Colorado," he recalls, "so I grew up with a certain familiarity with death. My maternal grandfather was a mortician ('undertaker' we called it then), and eventually my own father took over the business after attending mortuary science school in Chicago.

"I remember constantly pondering the questions I had concerning death: Where do dead people go? Do they just go into a hole in the ground? What does it feel like to be dead?

"One autumn day when I was about nine, I was sitting on a park bench behind the old mortuary building and pondering the last question. I tried to imagine where my Grandpa McHenry was—or *if* he still was—and what he was experiencing in death. I pictured in my mind a dark, lonely, black expanse of 'nothing and no one' forever and ever.

"A terrible and chilling dread came over my entire body. But then instantly it vanished. It was replaced by a warm, comfortable, and bright feeling—and a kind and loving presence. I seemed to hear my grandpa saying, 'See Stan, it's all right. I'm just in a place that's different.'

"From that day on," Stan remembers, "I never again had a fear of death. I *knew* that I would still 'be' after I died. It would just be different. Later, when I studied comparative religion at the University of Colorado, I resonated very strongly to the teachings of Eastern philosophy and reincarnation. Lately I have been trying to restore the spiritual nature that I strongly felt as a child."

Mystical Mathematics

Marty is a forty-seven-year-old actuarial consultant living in southern California. The oldest of three children, he grew up in a Catholic family that moved often because of his father's army position. Marty recalls: "When I was a second-grader in Catholic school, the teacher gave a homework assignment introducing the concept of zero. There were several problems in which zero was added to or subtracted from various numbers. Of course, the answer was that the number always remained the same.

"Most of my classmates regarded this fact as simply another of the innumerable rules to be memorized. They experienced no more perplexity than with any other arithmetic rule. But I sat alone in my room that night and stared with tears at the seemingly senseless problems.

"I wondered, 'How could I add something to a number and yet the number remain unchanged?' Suddenly, I *understood*— and had the first mystical experience of my life. The immensity of the concept of nothingness overwhelmed me. I was awed by the realization that mathematicians were brilliant enough to capture this immensity in a little symbol. I felt a sense of comfort and of light, and immediately decided to become a mathematician.

"Interestingly," Marty recollects, "I had another mystical experience involving mathematics at the age of thirteen. It was when I first studied the proof that the square root of two is irrational—not a fraction. This understanding too evoked a tremendous feeling of light and profound insight."

Having recently completed Jungian analytic training, Marty comments: "My religious beliefs are pretty typical for a Jungian—a deep belief, based on inner experience, in a higher power who takes an interest in our lives and is encountered daily in our dreams. I'm comfortable with others calling that power God, but I rarely use the term."

Gazing at the Stars

Amanda is a fifty-nine-year-old artist living in Asheville, North Carolina, and the mother of five children. She relates: "I grew up as the only child of a brutal, alcoholic mother and an indifferent father. One summer evening when I was about three years old, I was gazing at the stars in the nighttime sky and wondering about them.

"Suddenly a flash of knowledge came to me that my parents 'weren't the only boss of me.' There was someone or something that was 'in charge' of my life."

"Those were the exact words," Amanda remembers, "and at that young age I had no conception of God. I felt the awareness intensely and with absolute certainty. It was immensely comforting.

"That flashlike intuition became important to me because of the various traumas I experienced until I reached adolescence. Looking back today, it's clear that my inner spiritual knowledge helped to sustain me through a very difficult period of my life."

We're All Related

Jill is a forty-eight-year-old woman living in Stamford, Connecticut. Growing up in Los Angeles, she attended Methodist church sporadically, with little formal religious exposure. "One day when I was about six," recalls Jill, "I sat thinking about my relatives: how I was related to them, and how they were related to other people. I suddenly had the awareness that I could take those relationships all the way back to the first people. I then realized that I was related to every person on earth who had ever lived. This made me very happy to feel connected to everyone, and I hurried into the living room to tell my mother.

"I was brimming with joy," recollects Jill, "and had a very warm, full feeling in my heart. But my pleasure with this awareness fell on unaccepting ears. My mother's huffy response was 'Well, we're *not* related to the Chinese!' and then she abruptly walked away. I remember feeling sorry, rather than angry, that she didn't understand how we're all related."

"Stuck inside My Body"

Dorothy is a fifty-year-old machinist living in Kansas City. She grew up in Detroit as the younger of two children in a middle-class Catholic home. "My mother's motto in life was always,

'What will the neighbors think?' and I always felt slightly apart from my family members.

"One day when I was about four," Dorothy recalls, "I was standing just outside our kitchen door facing into the dining room. All of a sudden I became intensely aware that my body was just a temporary vehicle for the essence that is 'me.' With a very strange sensation, I felt that my body was giving me only a limited tunnel vision, and when disembodied I would again be able to see in all directions at once.

"Still with this strong awareness, I turned to my mother and said, 'Do you ever feel funny being stuck inside your body?'

"My mother glared at me with a totally uncomprehending expression and snapped, 'I don't know what you're talking about!' From her irritated look I could see that she really didn't.

"Today," comments Dorothy, "I often feel what a small blip this life is in the context of eternity—just as the earth is such a minute part of the universe. I like to try stepping back and seeing as much of the 'big picture' as I can. Most people I know can't—or won't—do this, but my experience as a small child helped to create my present viewpoint."

The Projection Booth of Life

John is a fifty-year-old psychology professor in the California State University system. The older of two brothers, he grew up in New Jersey and was raised in the Presbyterian church. "As a special treat for my seventh birthday," John recalls, "My dad rented a film projector and several films for children. Some were cartoons and some were nature documentaries. I was fascinated by the film projector, for I had never seen one before.

"Answering my eager questions, Dad explained the difference between live action and cartoons: that cartoons are successive photographs of drawings. When projected very rapidly, they blur and form the illusion of motion. Dad added that live-action movies are also illusions, in a sense, since they're composed of many, many separate images, called 'frames,' that appear to be moving.

"The next day I found myself alone on our sunlit porch and thinking about Dad's explanation. Using my limited vocabulary as a child, I intensely began to wonder: Is reality just a series of wholly separate experiences, connected to one another in rapid succession? Or is reality continuous, but our conscious experience of it is divided into segments? If so, what happens in between moments of experience?

"All at once, something happened. It's very hard to describe adequately," comments John. "I suddenly became fully aware of myself *'in the moment.'* Then I realized that some moments of experience are qualitatively different from others. Somehow, contemplating the nature of experience led me into an indescribable state in which I ceased to exist and yet I existed in a new, far more powerful way.

"This was truly a peak experience for me, and it definitely changed how I viewed my world," John observes. "Today I might say: Some rare moments consist of pure experience, there's nothing but the absoluteness of the experience itself. In this way, the tiny moment becomes timeless and eternal."

"I Am in Me"

Brittany is a twenty-three-year-old massage therapist living in rural Italy. The older of two sisters, she grew up in northern California in a nonreligious Protestant family. "One spring day when I was seven," Brittany recalls, "I was walking home from school and suddenly became fascinated by a phrase that popped into my mind: 'I am in me.'

"I began repeating the words silently in an effort to understand them. What tremendously intrigued me was the nature of my identity: this 'I' who observes and remembers from within this particular body, who looks out at the world through these particular eyes. Then I pondered about how this 'I' is always in motion—walking, passing by places and things, changing its physical perspective, even thinking.

"With this realization, I felt tremendously happy. In the ensuing days and weeks when I was alone, I would repeat these words over and over—'I am in me,'—and wonderfully enjoy the resultant feeling.

"After a while I tried telling a friend of mine about my insight. I asked if she had ever thought about being inside *oneself* instead of being inside the self of *another*. She looked at me with a bewildered expression, replied, 'I don't know what you're talking about,' and walked away.

"When I reached adolescence," Brittany relates, "I began spending more time with peers, and I thought less about such matters. More recently, my early experiences have become important again. They've given me a rich sense of personal spirituality independent of any institution or outside influence, and I'm grateful."

Thinking about Death and Eternity

Gary is a forty-eight-year-old computer scientist who has lived in southern California for most of his life. An only child, he was raised an Episcopalian and was active as an acolyte and choir member. "One evening when I was twelve, my parents and I were eating dinner at a local restaurant," Gary recalls. "Their conversation didn't concern me, and I sort of drifted away in my thoughts. I began to think about my ultimate destiny, and came to the realization of my death and how strange that concept was.

"Initially, I speculated about being dead and yet still conscious. This was an incredibly frightening concept. I rejected this horror as best as I could, but then was led to think more deeply about death and its consequences. The idea of infinity, eternity, grabbed me like a hideous monster: I wouldn't be dead for just fifty years, or a hundred years, or a thousand years . . . but forever. The sense of forever overwhelmed me, and I experienced a deep, personal terror. Only gradually did I became aware that my parents were calling to me, 'Gary? What's wrong? Gary, are you all right?'

"Apparently I had gone ashen in a very dramatic way and looked ill." Gary recollects. "For the next day or two I could do almost nothing but cry. Over the next weeks the thought would recur every few hours, and I would break into tears. Nothing could console me. If I saw the word 'death' or even anything related to it, I would fall into a crying spell. I began to miss a lot of school. A very difficult part of the ordeal was that I couldn't understand why everyone else in the world didn't feel as I did: how could *they* tolerate the idea of personal death? How could they function?

"This situation dragged on for several months, though the episodes began to diminish. Finally, my parents called our pastor and asked him to counsel me. He was a nice and obviously well-meaning man, and he described the afterlife to me as a sort of playground where my buddies and I would play together and just have a good time.

"His remarks seemed ludicrous to me. But strangely, I was so startled by his explanation that I experienced a kind of revelation. An inner voice that I hardly recognized assured me that the pastor's comments were indeed no answer at all, but that I had to be patient: I was still too immature to understand the truth. The voice emphasized that there really *is* an explanation about death, and if I waited, I would discover it and would like it.

"This voice within was so reassuring," Gary continues, "that I felt comforted and was able to dismiss the problem of death into my cosmic 'pending' file. I remained religious, but not so deeply committed to my own church. Finally, when I was nearly thirty years old, I was led to resume my spiritual quest."

Today Gary is deeply involved in studying comparative religion and mysticism. He observes: "The reality of my inner journey regarding death has always been with me. I now see myself as extremely fortunate to have had such a dramatic early experience in consciousness. It made me into an avid spiritual seeker and opened my horizons beyond what I now consider the valid, but limited, theology of mainstream church doctrine."

From Fear to Enlightenment

Victoria is a seventy-seven-year-old retired journalist living in Los Angeles. The fifth of seven children, she grew up on a farm in rural Ohio. Victoria's parents were nominally involved with the Presbyterian church, and she attended Sunday school. "When I was a small child," she recalls, "I loved life. I loved learning, and I loved being aware and alive. In our large family there was always someone to play with—lots of activity, but no real sense of closeness to any authority figures.

"One wintry day when I was about seven, two of my siblings and I were allowed to see a Saturday afternoon movie. On the same bill was a serial. It was called *The Fortieth Door*, a title I remember clearly after nearly seventy years. It was probably a ridiculous, amateurish film, in which various victims were imprisoned and murdered in a huge scary castle. It showed skeletons hanging from meat hooks, people drowning while a room filled with water.

"I was terrified. The movie triggered in me an obsessive fear, and the realization that all life ends in death struck me a stupefying blow. I couldn't understand how God could create anything as fascinating as life and at the same time make death inevitable. I thought it was sadistic. I became obsessed with the fear of death.

"One evening a few weeks after the movie," Victoria recollects, "I was lying in bed and trying to imagine the end of life: of not being alive. Is it nothingness, and if so, what is nothingness? It was impossible to imagine, and also frightening. So then I tried to imagine living forever . . . life as never ending. This was also impossible to imagine, but I was still attempting to 'experience' it in my mind.

"Suddenly, with a sort of burst of inner light, I felt life to be God and myself to be connected to God. It was a silent explosion. I understood that I was part of something loving and much, much greater than myself. It was not a thought but an ecstatically intense feeling.

"Since then," Victoria concludes, "I have felt as true the old adage that 'God is love.' In my view, living and behaving as if there is a loving God is certainly conducive to leading a life that's helpful to others."

Beyond All Memory

Pierre, the clinical psychologist whom we met in chapter 6, relates: "One day when I was three or four, I was playing alone in bushes around our house on a summer afternoon. My parents had several visitors, and they started arriving in expensive cars. I was watching it all from the bushes, and was seemingly undetected. Soon everyone had arrived, but I remained motionless in the bushes, enjoying the quietness and coziness of the spot.

"I first noticed that I could think about anything I wanted, and no one knew what it was," recalls Pierre. "As I conjured up memories to think about, I realized that I could go back only a short distance in time before I found myself beyond all memories and facing a total blankness.

"As I faced the blankness in my mind's eye, I gradually became aware that my identity transcended all these memories: that '*I*' *had no form or name, no history*, and filled this blankness or emptiness as an immensity extending to infinity. This awesome feeling lasted for several minutes, and then I became aware of myself as a little boy peering out of the bushes.

"I experienced a tremendous jolt—and a sense of regret mixed with anger and sadness—about having suddenly left my previous state of euphoric awareness. This memory has returned to me with increasing clarity as a result of my meditative practice. It still inspires me, how my usual childhood frame of mind was completely erased, and how I was able to merge with a much greater awareness."

"I've Been Here Before"

Anne is a fifty-eight-year-old woman living in Shreveport, Louisiana. She grew up with eight siblings. "At the age of about four," she recalls, "I found myself approaching a high counter in my mother's kitchen. As I reached the counter, I found myself entirely enveloped by light and heard a simple yet explosive thought within me: 'I've been here before!' Its feeling tone was peaceful and serene, but exact, like a statement of divine truth. None of my religious teaching had ever lent any support for my experience."

Five years later, Anne was playing boisterously one day with her brothers and sisters. As she came bursting through the back door, followed by others, "the same light, the same voice or thought came to me. It said, 'God has ordained you a husband, and he is out there in the world now as a little boy, as you are a little girl.' Those were the exact words."

Anne has been married for thirty-seven years. With three adult children and five grandchildren, she comments, "My family is my life." She and her husband share a strong spiritual sense that both trace back to their childhood years.

Singing about Identity

Edith is a forty-seven-year-old farmer who has spent most of her life in rural Missouri. The third of four children, Edith grew up in a nominally Catholic home. "When I was about four," she recalls, "I would lie on my back in bed and repeat over and over—almost like a chant or mantra—'I am me! I am me!'

"I would have the lovely sensation of sinking deeply into myself and would feel very much at peace with the world. I would also have a strong sense of God in those moments. In my adult life, there's no doubt that my search for God has been a search for the self that I think I knew intimately as a small child."

8

Within Religious Walls

All religions have one source.
                                          —WILLIAM BLAKE

W E have heard numerous reports from people whose most exalted moments of childhood occurred spontaneously. The particular triggers for such memorable events have been wide-ranging, involving exposure to nature on both a large and small scale, near-death or crisis phenomena, informal prayer, simple epiphanies of everyday life, and even philosophical musings. One might therefore conclude that organized religion is at best irrelevant, and at worst detrimental, to the nurturing of our highest sensitivities in early life.

This notion is not supported, however, by my research. Many individuals have recounted acutely meaningful, even ecstatic, childhood experiences that took place during worship services or the reading of Scripture. To be sure, a few vividly recall being misunderstood or criticized by poorly qualified religious teachers for relating such personal events, but this fact hardly invalidates the religious traditions those teachers represent. Instead, such instances raise the question: How do we revitalize religious training so that it truly nourishes rather than suppresses the child's innate spirituality?

126

The Biblical Verse

Marcy is a thirty-nine-year-old systems administrator living in Washington, D.C. She grew up on Long Island, where she attended a Protestant community church. "I had been going to Sunday school for several years," Marcy recalls, "and it was interesting, but nothing really dramatic ever happened. Then, one Sunday during class, I read Deuteronomy 6:4:

> Hear, O Israel: The Lord our God is one LORD
> and you shall love the LORD your God with all your heart,
> and with all your soul, and with all your might.
> And these words which I command you this day shall be
> Upon your heart.

"The words shot through me like a knife," Marcy remembers. "I was tremendously moved. We had never studied this passage in class before, and my family almost never discussed the Bible at home. Yet I *knew* that I had heard these words somewhere before—a previous incarnation, perhaps? Whatever the source of my sensation, that day in Sunday school—those biblical words—constituted a turning point in my young life. Leaving the classroom, I knew then that personal faith (if not organized religion) was going to play an important role in my life, and it has.

When Marcy was nineteen, she had another mystical experience, which occurred during a visit to the Grand Canyon. "Today my faith in the universe has not wavered," Marcy observes. "It started years ago with those words from Deuteronomy, and has grown stronger through the years. I firmly believe that no faith is possible without a personal experience of the transcendent, and I'm thankful for my own encounter with divine grace."

Baptist Confirmation

Matt is a fifty-nine-year-old counselor and ordained Baptist minister living in rural Indiana. He was raised in a conservative Baptist home with moderate religious involvement. "When I was fifteen, it was time for me to receive confirmation," Matt recalls. "I was standing in church with the others my age, not feeling anything particularly unusual.

"But as I went forward to profess my faith in Jesus as my savior, I had an unexpressible sensation, as though I had been uplifted beyond time and space. I felt myself walking with a new consciousness that made everything around me different. When the deacons took us back in the church to record our decisions, I waited for someone to tell me what was happening to me.

"Putting all that information down on the card seemed totally trivial. When the pastor came into the room, I waited expectantly as he expressed his joy in our decisions, told us when we would be baptized, and then prayed with us. My counselor shook my hand, and the room was empty.

"As I sat there waiting alone, I felt myself becoming transported again. I felt peaceful, joyous, and in touch with something vaster than I could conceive. Finally, I went to meet my parents. When I related my experience to others who were already church members, I was disappointed to find no one who had the slightest idea of what I was talking about."

Matt has experienced other timeless states since then. He emphasizes, however: "Only when I left the institutional church and began to read about mysticism did I discover the vocabulary I needed to describe my teenage experience. I do a lot of reading today on Christian mysticism and am currently writing a book on spiritual counseling."

Catholic Mass

Theresa is a forty-six-year-old journalist living in rural Kentucky. Having attended Catholic school as a youngster, she recalls: "This meant that daily Mass was a prerequisite before each day of classroom studies. As was the custom, our particular class would line up, two children at a time, and tread the familiar route to the old church next door where we attended services.

"One late winter morning during Mass, I suddenly felt conscious of a great distance that seemed to separate me from something. It was similar to seeing through a long, dark tunnel and being barely able to distinguish what was in the light at the other end. My entire physical reality became almost nonexistent, as I found myself focusing totally within. It was a very peaceful, blissful state."

"In the next instant," Theresa recollects, "I was again aware of my physical body, but as if for the first time. I felt strange, as though I had just been deposited somehow into this perimeter of flesh. In amazement, I wriggled my fingers and moved my arms up and down. I felt totally bewildered as to how I could be this physical and sensitized entity.

"So immersed was I in this puzzling phenomenon that I blurted to my line partner, Suzy, 'Do you ever wonder how you can be *you?*'

"Suzy obviously didn't share my sense of awe, for she looked at me with a baffled expression and replied, 'You think stupid!'

"I don't recall how much longer my sense of wonderment lasted after that cutting remark from my peer," comments Theresa today. "But I often wonder: Did I at that long-ago moment during Mass catch a fleeting glimpse of Soul? Or was

it a memory of some experience before I became the person
that is now me?"

Episcopal Mass

Ian is a thirty-eight-year-old transportation coordinator living
in rural North Carolina. He attended Episcopal church in
Pennsylvania as a child. "Inside the church, the tall wooden
ceiling arched high over my head," Ian recalls, "and was
darkened from years of incense. Dim red lights hung on black
chains from the cross-beams, indicating to visitors that the
sacraments were present. Every time the Mass was said, God
would make His presence known to me. I believed that I could
actually hear His voice."

"Another part of my faith and worship style was nurtured
at this same church. It was usually dark and still, smelling of
old incense and filled with memories. Its physical presence was
a tremendous spur for my praying and meditating when I
came and sat there alone. I didn't realize it at the time, but by
sitting and staring at the cross on the altar I was actually using
an ancient form of Eastern meditation to still my mind. In this
way I could better hear the small, quiet voice that speaks to us
all with such authority."

Tears of Joy

Hillary, the schoolteacher living in Nepal whom we met in
chapter 3, relates: "At the age of twelve I would often accompany my parents to church and listen intently to the minister's
sermon. I would think, 'If only we could all be as good as he's
asking us to be, what a wonderful world it would be!'

"What would surprise and puzzle me, however, was that when we sang a hymn, I would choke up and feel like crying. I think it stemmed from an overwhelming sense of goodness—wanting everyone to be good—yet knowing that most people would return to their habitual patterns of behavior upon leaving church.

"Sometimes I actually had to stop my singing, for fear of visibly crying and then embarrassedly having to explain the strange emotion. Maybe these were tears of a type of happiness or joy, for I felt very close to my parents, and very secure, when sitting in church during those moments."

"These Are My People"

Margaret is an eighty-five-year-old English woman living in London. She recalls: "At the age of ten I made a first visit to a Quaker religious service. I instantly knew, with absolute surety, that this was my *spiritual home* and that these Friends were *my people*. I felt certain of God's presence and love, and a wonderful sense of trust possessed me."

Margaret comments: "Through all the many years and trials of my life, that childhood moment has remained strong with me. Though it's harder for me to get around due to my age, I'm still quite involved with the Society of Friends here in London."

Greek Orthodox Icon

Harvey is a thirty-nine-year-old communications consultant living in suburban Philadelphia. Having grown up Catholic in New York City, he recalls: "One Sunday, when I was about eight, my father and I visited a Greek Orthodox church, rather than attend our regular Mass. When I entered the unfamiliar building a few blocks from our home, my attention was instantly captivated by a huge Jesus Pantocrator icon. I was enthralled, for it seemed to possess a tremendous force and power.

"Like a great and magnificent rock," Harvey recounts, "the memory of that icon has weighed upon my psyche to this day. Whenever I remember that childhood event, it's always in the form of a wordless watching: a kind of contemplation that thrives in the absence of spoken words.

"Mother Tessa Bielicki has described such contemplation as 'iconic looking,' which provides a long, loving look at the real. In *Behold the Beauty of the Lord: Praying with Icons*, Henri Nouwen explains that icons aren't easy to 'see' or to comprehend immediately. 'It's only gradually, after a patient, prayerful presence that they start speaking to us. And as they speak, they speak more to our inner than our outer senses. They speak to the heart that searches for God.' "

Harvey adds: "This has certainly been true for me. My childhood encounter with the icon of Jesus powerfully ignited my life's spiritual journey. I'm only now realizing that I've passed through several meaningful phases in which God has been present in various ways. I view my present task as recovering these moments as vital and intimate dialogue."

The Dream of Life

Shannon is a forty-seven-year-old publishing manager living in Philadelphia. The oldest of seven children, she was raised in a middle-class Catholic environment. "We went to parochial school," Shannon recalls, "and I felt very religious. I would kneel before statues of the Blessed Virgin and intensely pray, especially that I didn't want to sin. I loved the whole atmosphere of the chapel services during Mass or benediction: the carved wooden walls, pews and special boxes, the odor of incense, the Gregorian chants.

"One day when I was about seven, I was kneeling as usual in the chapel. For some reason, I started to wonder whether I was really asleep and just dreaming that I was kneeling there, or whether I was truly awake. Was my life a dream? Or was it real? Who was I if I was only dreaming this life?"

Shannon comments: "Ever since that moment, I've known that there's something else to life than mere outward reality. It was in my twenties that I first read the famous Chinese parable about the monk who dreamed he was a butterfly, and then wondered if he was also a butterfly dreaming that he was a monk. When I first read the parable, it reminded me exactly of my experience in the chapel.

"Whenever I pray or meditate," Shannon concludes, "I still seek the true self somehow glimpsed in that wondrous moment of childhood."

The Dazzling Light

Rita is a forty-year-old dispatcher who has spent most of her life in the Chicago area. The fourth of five children, she was raised in a Catholic family and attended parochial school. "One day our class was saying morning prayers," Rita recalls, "and we began the Hail Mary. Soon after starting to pray, I experienced a dazzling light forming before my eyes. The light grew and grew until it encompassed all of my vision. It was as bright as the sun, except I could gaze straight into it.

"I was awestruck. The light generated limitless peace and

love. I was about to let myself go into the light, when I suddenly heard the nun screaming my name. Apparently, she had been calling to me repeatedly, with the whole class staring at me.

"When I finally responded, I was escorted to the Mother Superior's office. The nuns whispered among themselves in hushed voices, and I was required to sit for an hour in the Mother Superior's office under her strict gaze. She never told my family of the episode."

Longing to Worship

Mildred is a seventy-one-year-old woman who has spent most of her life in central Pennsylvania. The older of two sisters, Mildred grew up nominally exposed to Catholicism. "On Sunday mornings when I was five, my mother and I would take the trolley to visit her parents. We would pass a large and beautiful stone building. For some reason I considered the building—Trinity United Methodist Church—to be the most beautiful I had ever seen. When weather was warm, the church windows were opened, and as I stood on the sidewalk, I could hear a mighty pipe organ and melodic strains of people singing.

"The music stirred me deeply. Each time we passed the church, I would say, 'When I get big enough to do what I want to do, I'm going to join that church.'

"Because my parents attended no church," Mildred recalls, "I had no idea why I was having such strong feelings for this church, especially since I knew nothing about Methodism.

"Several months passed. I became friends with four neighborhood girls who all attended the church, and I managed to persuade my mother to let me attend too. The following

Sunday the rain was falling very hard, and I thought my mother would back out. But curiously enough, she didn't.

"On that Sunday I definitely found what I had been seeking. I was placed in the beginner's class and given a tiny card called a Memory Verse. To my surprise, it said: 'God is Love.' The following Sunday my father also decided to attend, and both my parents eventually became active members."

Mildred comments: "Those neighborhood girls became my lifelong friends, though one died a few years ago. Today another is celebrating her fiftieth wedding anniversary, as my husband and I did this year. Happy are our memories of old Trinity Church, though I still wonder why God chose to speak to me. Perhaps, as it is written in the Bible, 'a little child shall lead them.' "

The Bar Mitzvah Ceremony

David is a youthful sixty-three-year-old tour operator who grew up in Philadelphia. The older of two sons of Jewish immigrants, he lives in New Jersey. Concerning his bar mitzvah, David recalls: "I was up on the platform of the synagogue, with my family and relatives below in the audience. As I was called to read the Torah, I suddenly felt I was becoming a different person, or that I was being enlarged within and linked up to all those who had lived before me and studied and read the Torah too. With intense emotion, I then made a speech that I had written myself. I implored God to make me a good man, and I meant it.

David comments: "Far beyond my youthful expectation, the ceremony was an utterly powerful experience. Though I've never been ritualistic in my Jewish involvement, this childhood episode remains a foundation for my entire spiritual life."

"God Isn't Like That!"

Gene is a thirty-six-year-old man living in Seattle. As a child he attended Sunday school at a Lutheran church in the area. "I was about eight," Gene recalls, "when one day, our Sunday school teacher gave a lecture about eternal hell and damnation as the punishment for all those who fail to become baptized. It was a very disturbing and upsetting subject for all of us. At the lecture's conclusion, one girl asked, 'How about the people in China and India who have never heard of Jesus? Are they all going to hell?' I had never liked the girl, but I'll always be grateful to her for asking that question.

"The teacher smiled deprecatingly and said, 'Well, that just points out our responsibility toward mission work.' Having said this, he made his escape.

"At that point my awareness of the others in the room faded. I looked down at the table before me, with its books and papers, and lost sight of them and everything else. My fists were clenched in my lap under the table. Suddenly I heard in my mind a voice that sounded like mine, but it had far more power and conviction than I ever could have consciously mustered. Shouting within me, it said, 'God isn't such a mean old bugger!'

"I instantly reawakened to the room with its people and things. For a moment I was afraid that I had shouted the words aloud. No one was paying particular attention to me, however, so I concluded that I hadn't engaged in open outburst."

Over the ensuing years Gene has become keenly interested in mysticism and is still puzzled by his early experience. "How can I explain the energy of that voice? It sounded like my own," he comments, "yet it carried more strength, certainty, and conviction than possessed by my eight-year-old self. Was it recall of life before birth? A message from 'the self' or 'the higher self,' as some like to say? An inspiration from God? Whatever the source, the experience means something important to me."

Beam from the Heart

Marian is a fifty-one-year-old supervisor for a county mental health agency in southern California. She was raised in a Catholic family and recalls: "I must have been about three years old when I was in church one day with my mother. She was kneeling beside me on the kneeler, her hands folded on the back of the pew, her lips silently praying, and her eyes gazing at the altar. I was standing next to her, just about eye level, and quietly watching her.

"Mother turned to me and smiled, and then lovingly put her arm around me. As she faced the altar to resume her prayers, I suddenly saw a golden beam of light emanate from the area of her heart. The light traveled to the altar's center, then to my heart, and then went back to hers.

"I don't recall having any thoughts about the experience, but I liked it very much and knew that it was good. Today," Marian adds, "I'm active nationally as well as locally with the mainline Protestant church. At work I consider myself a 'change agent,' and am committed to ending world hunger and creating peace. My early experience in church that day remains important as a source of personal inspiration."

9

Uncanny Perceptions

Then the eyes of the blind shall be opened.
—ISAIAH 36:5

I T has long been a tradition in both Eastern and Western religions that childhood harbors a special sensitivity to the mysteries of human existence. Great sages throughout the world have considered the openness of children to be a special gateway to transcendental experience. Lacking the adult's tendency to see and feel things through the dull guise of habit, children are often more able to apprehend reality directly, rather than merely philosophize about it.

As mystical adepts have taught in many cultures, our daily life resembles sleepwalking. It is the central task of each of us to wake up from our inner slumber. To do this effectively means to learn to trust our own perceptions, yet, as we leave our early years, this simple act becomes increasingly difficult. Self-doubt makes us timid and eventually even fearful about accepting the validity of what we feel and experience. Instead of listening to the "still small voice" within, we follow the clamor around us.

This important notion is beautifully conveyed by the nine-teenth-century Danish folklorist Hans Christian Andersen. In his simple but powerful fairy tale, "The Emperor's New

Clothes," many in the great kingdom plainly see that their ruler is naked. But afraid of being branded as simpletons, they are unwilling to trust their own eyes and instead join in the chorus of lavish praise for the king's sartorial elegance. It takes an innocent child to exclaim the truth, and then *everyone* (interestingly, beginning with the child's father) feels secure to do so.

With this perspective, let us turn to the intriguing reports that follow. To paraphrase Shakespeare, they underscore that mainstream philosophy hardly contains all that exists within heaven and earth.

"A Rushing, Mighty Wind"

Catherine, the retired schoolteacher whom we met in chapter 2, recounts: "In 1907, when my family emigrated from England to British Columbia, my maternal grandmother reacted very emotionally and was particularly distressed at being parted from my mother. Thereupon, my mother sincerely promised that if grandmother was ever in need, they would promptly return to England to visit her. This promise may have been rash, but it was not lightly made.

"Two years later," Catherine remembers, "my grandfather cabled that grandmother had suffered a stroke. As promised earlier, my parents immediately began preparations to visit. But a second cable brought news of Grandmother's death.

"My mother took it very badly. She said little, but was clearly anguished about having been unable to keep the promise to her mother.

"A few days passed. It was midwinter, and the rural Canadian countryside was deep in snow. I was three years old and sleeping on a cot in my parents' bedroom. At about 4:00 A.M.

we were suddenly awakened by the commotion of a violent wind, which seemed to fill the whole house. It sounded like a herd of bellowing, braying animals, and I was frightened. The noise didn't last long—only a minute or two, perhaps—but swept continuously through the house, and then ceased as suddenly as it had begun.

"Within a few moments, my older brother and sister burst into the room. They too were scared and demanded to know what had caused the commotion. Father reluctantly went downstairs to put on his heavy overcoat and headgear, and told us to stay put. Oddly, my mother wasn't at all afraid, but curiously, seemed quite happy.

"Our family waited in silence until father returned, looking puzzled. He related, 'There's been no snowfall from the roof, and there are no marks at all on the ground.' Through the frosty window, we could see that it was a clear, starlit night, and there was no apparent wind. Mother suggested that we all go back to bed.

"The next morning father called at each neighboring ranch within a mile of us and asked whether any of them had similarly been disturbed by a roaring wind during the night. No one had. They all agreed that it had been a fine, still night. At breakfast my older brother persistently asked about the rushing commotion. Then mother said she would explain what it meant to her.

"She took a Bible from the bookshelf and read aloud from the Acts of the Apostles (2:1–2):

When the day of Pentecost had come, they were all together in one place. And suddenly a sound came from heaven like the rush of a mighty wind, and it filled all the house where they were sitting.

" 'That's what we heard,' mother quietly explained, 'the sound of a mighty, rushing wind.'" She said that Grandmother had come to tell us that she was all right, and that she (mother) was grateful for the unusual experience."

Catherine comments: "From that day onward, mother seemed restored to her happy self, and the experience has always left with me a strong spiritual feeling about life and death. Much later, as an adult, I realized that what mother had told us wasn't in any way unnatural. The incident was never discussed afterward, except once by my father in his last years."

Music of the Soul

Helen, the instructional technologist whom we met in chapter 5, relates: "I was about ten when my grandfather died, and the following night I slept in the same room with my grandmother. Although she and my mother were both very sad, I had no sense that grandfather's death was something disastrous or unnatural. That is, no one was panicking or seemed to need any particular reassurance.

"That night I awoke very suddenly. My mind was clear and alert. This was not, nor has it ever been, how I usually awaken. I saw the alarm clock beside grandmother's bed: 3:15 A.M. I saw our quiet, moonlit yard through the window.

"Then I distinctly felt my grandfather's presence in an almost indefinable way. It's very hard to describe. It was as though he were speaking to me, and yet was within me. It seemed that I was like a musical instrument that Grandfather was gently using to materialize, or give form to, his thoughts for me, in the way that his voice and my ears had functioned in the past.

"What was Grandfather communicating? He encouraged me to assure Mom and Grandma that he was fine, that everything was fine. Grandfather related many other things that I couldn't remember well the next day, but his message of well-being was clear. The last things I remember are seeing that the clock was at 4:00 A.M., and feeling myself falling soundly asleep as immediately as I had awakened."

Helen comments: "None of this seemed strange, and I experienced no fear, only peace and harmony. Ever since, I've had a very comforting and secure feeling about what we perceive as death."

Double Self-Awareness

Anna is a seventy-year-old retired administrator for an international relief agency. The youngest of three children, she was born in England, where she was raised a Christian Scientist. "One morning when I was about five," Anna recalls, "I awoke and sat up in my bed. All of a sudden, very distinctly, I saw myself sitting at the foot of the bed. The other 'me' was my mirror image in every respect. More strangely, the consciousness that was 'I' was not restricted to either of the two girls, but *moved between them* until finally it stayed with the child at the head of the bed. The 'me' then solidified somehow and the other child disappeared.

"The little child who remained—me—slid down under the covers. I felt no fear or discomfort, no after feeling of abnormality. It seemed like a natural occurrence at the time, yet I've remembered it all my life.

"As I've grown older," Anna reflects, "I've given the experience more thought. To me, Mind or God is a consciousness—and a power—that isn't mine or me, but of which I'm nonetheless a part, and that can be called upon to operate in my life, though I can't dictate its operation. I remain strongly interested in the study of consciousness research, self-observation, and physics—to the extent that I can understand these!"

"Ask Them to Tell You the Opposite"

Joan is a fifty-two-year-old speech pathologist who lives in the Boston area. A divorced mother of three children, she grew up in Philadelphia as an only child in her mother's second marriage. Joan's mother and father were Episcopalian and Catholic respectively, but rarely attended church. When she reached the age of five, Joan learned the shocking secret that she had three much older half siblings from her mother's first marriage, all living in foster care. Soon after learning this secret, Joan began to experience the pleasant companionship of an imaginary playmate named "Mr. Goodman."

"He was an old man with a long, white beard," Joan recounts, "and it seems that he was often with me, whatever I was doing. We talked together a lot, but I remember now the specific content of only one conversation.

"It was at an ordinary mealtime with all the family members around the table. Mr. Goodman was crouched under the table, as he had often done before, and he was giving me advice. He told me, 'Tell your family members that if they want you to do something, they must tell you the *opposite*.'

"For example," Joan relates, "If my parents wanted me to drink milk, they were supposed to tell me, "Joan, *don't* drink milk.' He reminded me on several occasions to relay this information to my parents, and I did so."

Exactly what effect did the intriguing Mr. Goodman have

on Joan's childhood? "I'm not certain," she comments, "but many years later, I imagine today that the purpose might have been to give me a modest sense of power or control in a chaotic childhood. If so, then the inner strategy worked."

The Mysterious Name

Melanie is a thirty-eight-year-old social worker living on Long Island. She relates: "Since the age of about fifteen months, my younger son, Adam, has continuously addressed or referred to his older brother, Jason, as Dovi (pronounced *Duhvy*). We're Jewish, but that's not anything like Jason's real Hebrew name. Initially, we thought Adam just had articulation difficulty, but he's now almost three years old and pronounces other *J* sounds and *J* names very well. Often, Adam likes to address his brother as Dov, as it's affectionately abbreviated today in Israel.

"My husband and I never called Jason anything but his real name. Nor does our family know any children named Dovi or Dov. As far as we know, Adam had never met a child with this name. He knows nothing about Hebrew or Israeli names.

"Until recently," Melanie continues, "Adam would also refer to himself as Sekh when asked his name by family acquaintances. Perhaps he was mispronouncing the name Seth. Anyway, by now even I address Jason as Dovi in a nickname, as do several neighborhood children.

"What is interesting, too, is that from the age of barely one year, Adam has been unusually solicitous and concerned about Jason's whereabouts at all times. Sometimes he would scold or correct Jason in the manner of someone much older—not as barely a toddler! The upshot is that I've become convinced, as has my husband, that Adam knows Jason from a previous existence in Israel, and was his mentor in some personal way. We wonder whether he'll always address him as Dovi. I guess only time will tell."

"My Mirror Image"

Carolyn, the fifty-three-year-old Springfield, Illinois, woman whom we met in chapter 3, was an only child, and by the age of three or four she regularly experienced the companionship of an imaginary playmate. "She was very real to me," recalls Carolyn. "Actually, when I looked at her, she was a mirror image of myself.

"We played together early mornings and at bedtimes a great deal. She told me that her name was Carolyn Beatik or Beatrice Johnson, and that she had died in the Great Earthquake of San Francisco.

"I remember getting very agitated with my mother one Sunday evening. When mother came to check on me to see if I had gone to sleep, I asked her if she could see the little girl. Mother uttered an emphatic no.

"I told mother that my girlfriend was standing there right next to her. Then I asked mother to leave the room, as we were playing. We carried on many conversations, my mirror image friend and me."

Radiant Balls of Light

Heather is a thirty-two-year-old woman who grew up in a middle-class New Jersey family as the older of two children. Though outwardly respectable, Heather's childhood upbringing was marked by physical and sexual abuse by her father. Like several other respondents in this book, however, Heather was able to cope with such abuse in an important inner manner.

"A time of true sanctuary for me," she recalls, "was the period before I fell asleep. Beginning around age four, I used to get into bed, and as I fell asleep I would wait for what I thought of as 'my lights'—absolutely gorgeous golden flecks of falling and moving light that would appear before me in my room.

"It was like a shower of mica in the sunlight," Heather recollects, "except these gold lights would change colors as they fell as softly as powdery snow. They would reverse and change direction—first downward, then to the side, and then up and around again.

"The feelings I experienced as I watched these golden flecks were like a miracle in my fear-dominated life: indescribable comfort and peace. It was like falling asleep at the breast of the most loving mother imaginable."

Heather initially described these ethereal images to her mother, who "saw them as a problem induced by insufficient bedroom window shades and immediately bought me heavier shades. The next day she asked me if I still saw the lights, and I answered yes. On the third day a second set of room-darkening, opaque shades were installed. When questioned the next morning if I still saw lights, I once more answered yes. I could tell that my mother was frustrated and upset, so I never mentioned the golden flecks again. I could tell they weren't a subject to be discussed with her."

These experiences diminished and then ceased altogether by adolescence. But, Heather comments, "when I feel upset or just overcome by something, I call on the memory of those beautiful lights. It's still a great comfort and uplift to me."

Witnessing Grandmother's Death

Roslyn, the retired schoolteacher whom we met in chapter 2, fondly relates: "My maternal grandmother was my special friend. The two of us shared the same bedroom in the cramped apartment that my parents rented in New York City.

"Grandmother was a deeply spiritual person, whose Roman Catholic faith sustained and energized her life. We had wonderful times together, going for walks in our neighborhood park and talking about all sorts of things. Then, when I was ten, grandmother became extremely ill.

"One day soon after, my father was sitting at her bedside and I was standing at the foot of her bed. My mother and the rest of the family were quietly talking in the dining room. I remember thinking that they were absenting themselves from an awesome occasion.

"Grandmother struggled for breath for a long while. Then her frail body relaxed as she approached the end. It was very strange, for the only way I can describe it is, it was as though grandmother had slipped out of the room into a greater realm. At that moment I was acutely aware of the presence of the mysterious realm."

For Roslyn, "the experience of witnessing my beloved grandmother's death profoundly affected my view of human existence. I never forgot the importance that religious faith had for her. At the same time, I became keenly aware of the transitory quality of our lives and all that we cherish.

"As I've gotten older and retired professionally, I've become more interested in the role of mysticism in religion. I read the Bible a great deal now, especially because I had so little exposure to it when I was young."

"Come, See the Beautiful Lady!"

Lana is a sixty-two-year-old retired office worker living in the Chicago area. The second-oldest in an Irish-Catholic family, she grew up in Philadelphia. "My father had muscular dystrophy and was an armchair tyrant. His first response to any request was 'No!'

"One evening when I was about four, I excitedly called my parents and aunts to 'come upstairs and see the beautiful lady.' I was spellbound by the sight. Upon my second or third insistence, they came to my room, and of course, they couldn't see anything. They assumed that I was lying," comments Lana, "and dubbed me a liar for years afterward."

Antebellum Time Warp

Jane is a forty-four-year-old free-lance writer living in Charlotte, North Carolina. The younger of two children, she was raised a Catholic in suburban Milwaukee. "It was a peaceful environment," Jane recalls, "and a simpler time, with Dutch elms arched over the streets and sidewalks for strolling or riding bikes. The two- and three-story houses were set a few yards apart from one another.

"One cool autumn evening some friends and I were playing hide-and-seek. We ran across streets and into yards to find hiding places. Taking off from the others, I found myself between two houses a block from my home: familiar territory.

"But suddenly I was no longer a short, redhaired fourteen-year-old girl living in the 1950s. I was an eight-year-old black slave boy. I watched my grandfather, whom I loved a lot, tilling in the fields and whistling a tune.

"I can't say how much time passed," recalls Jane. "It might

have been an instant, or hours. I couldn't explain what had just transpired, and I knew people would think me crazy if I tried.

"At the age of nineteen, I read *The Search for Bridey Murphy*, and it greatly aroused my curiosity about reincarnation. Over the years, the topics of mysticism, metaphysics, and the unknown have become major interests in my life. I now believe that there's a reason for everything, and that the universe works perfectly."

Looking Down from the Ceiling

Jason, a seventy-eight-year-old film producer, relates: "My father was a gifted storyteller, and when he was home from his business travels, he would tell a continuing saga to my two sisters and me. Father would sit in a straight-backed chair, and we would sit cross-legged on the floor and look up at him.

"He would tell us about the adventures of three frontier children and their Native American friend, and how they all met and then conquered various problems together. We would sit spellbound.

"At some point in the story, on several occasions, I would feel an indescribable, internal click, sounding like the click of a toy cricket when you press the steel bottom and the dimple in it makes a sound.

"Instantly, I would feel myself high above the group. I would be looking down and seeing all four of us, as though staring through the wrong end of a telescope.

"The story would continue, and then abruptly I would be a boy looking up at his father again. I wondered about this puzzling phenomenon, but never told anyone nor asked anyone older for an explanation."

Jason comments: "The experiences gave me a lifelong interest in spiritual healing and metaphysics, and my success as a filmmaker has been to produce films and videotapes dealing with medical and scientific themes."

The Luminous Globe

Hilda is a sixty-eight-year-old retired metallurgical technician living in Hot Springs, Arkansas. "I was about twelve," she recalls, "and was spending the night with my maternal grandmother. The day before, my paternal grandfather had been severely injured at the county fair and was in the hospital. I had visited him earlier that day.

"That night I went to bed in the guest room as usual and turned the light off. But instead of darkness, there was a light in the room. I looked up and was startled to see a luminous globe hovering near me. Instantly, I knew that my grandfather had died. I heard no voice and felt no fear. Nor was I upset, and I guess I eventually drifted off to sleep.

"Early the next morning, when everyone was still sleeping, the downstairs telephone rang. As my grandmother woke up to answer it, I told her, 'Grandpa died last night.'

"She said, 'Don't be silly!' and went to answer the telephone. When grandmother came back, she stood in amazement and softly said, 'How did you know that?'

"I replied, 'I just knew.'

"I didn't want to describe the luminous globe to her or to anyone else, because it seemed too weird. In fact," Hilda comments, "I told no one about the experience until fairly recently, after learning that other people have had similar encounters and were sharing them with others."

The Face of Tranquillity

Laurie is a thirty-one-year-old photography assistant who has spent most of her life in Seattle. The second-born of four children, she grew up in a nominally Episcopal home. "My parents never talked about religion," Laurie emphatically recalls, "but I often had conversations about God with my grandfather. I was ten years old when I saw him for the last time.

"Grandfather became very ill and was in a local hospital. When I entered his room to visit, I saw him half propped up in bed and looking out the window. Though certainly no one had told me, I knew it would be the last time I would ever see this wonderful man alive. I sat alone with my grandfather as he placed his trembling hand flat against the glass. My small fingers lined up with his, and the window seemed to disappear.

"Grandfather didn't speak, but he smiled at me with a calm, gentle, tranquil expression. A mood of total peace came over his face. I sensed that he wouldn't be alive much longer and felt that somehow he was communicating this in a reassuring manner.

"Then suddenly I was seeing not my grandfather but another man who had the same gentle look on his face and a light around his head.

"When he spoke, his words were soft and kind: 'Keep your hands open, my little one, for I shall fill them up.'

"Then the vision disappeared, and I saw my grandfather's weak, gently tranquil face once more.

"He died the next morning. In the grief I felt throughout the next year, this experience stayed with me, and gave me a strong spiritual connection that remains to the present day."

Cellular Awareness

Janie is a forty-seven-year-old psychologist living in Greens-boro, North Carolina. The older of two daughters, she grew up without religious affiliation in southern California. "I was about twelve," Janie recalls, "and one day after school, I was lying on my bed. I was reading a book about the human body—especially, blood cells and physical anatomy. I felt myself becoming more and more fascinated by the subject.

"Suddenly it was as though I *became* all the things I was reading about. I could see and feel the blood cells in my veins, my heart beating, my muscles stretching.

"It's difficult to describe, but it was like I became something not my body but a thing apart—something that was able to be inside and watch my body processes functioning. My consciousness was not the same as my body but something separate.

"I thought that this was a really neat experience and wanted to tell someone. But at the time," Janie continues, "I had no close friends and didn't get along well with my parents. So I told no one about the episode, which greatly deepened my interest in biology and nature. In a way that's hard to describe, it also made me feel like I belonged somewhere and was a part of something larger.

"As I grew older and had other experiences of oneness with nature, I've become convinced that our consciousness is much more powerful and all-encompassing than what we're usually taught."

Tumbling into the Void

Denise is a forty-one-year-old yoga teacher living in Dallas, Texas. "I grew up in an affluent and nonreligious family," she recalls. "During times alone in my room, I would often 'tumble back' into another reality—focusing on what was here before the universe or anything else existed. I would tumble further and further into this secure void, relishing the feeling of quiet detachment, almost floating."

Denise comments: "I never told anyone of these episodes. Somehow I knew that my inner tumbling was not an ordinary thought process but a special experience that occurred only when I was alone for a while. I was certainly not scientifically motivated during these inner journeys. I never actually *thought* about space, time, or the universe's creation. That is, my 'tumbling back' experiences were much stronger and involved richer sensations than mere thinking.

"These experiences just happened naturally. There was no particular trigger like art, music, or exposure to nature," Denise adds. "More than thirty years later, I recall these episodes with great fondness, awe, and reverence. They left me with a feeling of connectedness with whatever is beyond my own reality, and the knowledge that I could change my ordinary state of consciousness."

Preview of World War II

Dolores is a sixty-year-old professor at the University of Utah. The fifth of six children in a Mormon family, she spent her first years in Idaho. "One morning I was in the basement of our home and started to ascend the stairs. Suddenly it seemed as if a small window appeared on the wall, although it was an inside wall. As though I was watching a movie projected onto it, I saw men and armies and airplanes and such. I never shared this vision with anyone, but years later came to regard it as a precognition of World War II.

"It may also relate to a later experience I had as a teenager during the war. I stood alone near our house in Atherton, California, and witnessed hundreds of airplanes flying overhead in a westerly direction, obviously headed for the war effort."

Dolores comments: "Whether because of the 'movie' vision or not, I always felt a childhood connection to the All that Is, and experienced a real sense of peace in nature. I'm no longer a member of the Mormon church, but consider myself a keeper of the personal faith. God, to me, is creative energy, and I see all life as participating in this envelope of energy."

Shifting Inner Size

Nora is a forty-five-year-old woman living on Long Island, New York. "Many times during childhood," she recalls, "while resting or before sleep, I felt myself entering an intense inner state, in which I felt that I was the smallest speck in the universe. I also felt as though I were the largest person in the world.

"At first I excitedly told others about these experiences, but people had no idea what I was talking about. Of course, I also had a difficult time explaining what I meant. Eventually I stopped discussing these sensations."

Nora comments: "Sometimes I have tried to recapture this feeling as an adult. I have been successful, fleetingly, maybe two or three times."

Time Warp: The Old American West

Kim, the young Australian woman whom we met in chapter 4, recounts: "One day when I was nine, I was quietly playing outside my house as usual. Suddenly I felt myself plunged into a profoundly real daydream.

"The time period was of the early pioneer settlers of the American West, involving a family of two children and their parents. With absolute clarity I saw the image of a mother and daughter on a veranda waving good-bye to the father and son. They were sitting on a wagon filled with their furniture. When I saw the roughly clothed son, I knew that somehow it was me.

"Even though the episode lasted only a few seconds," remembers Kim, "I distinctly knew that this family was in the midst of hard times. They were selling their furniture to obtain income."

Kim experienced the identical daydream several times later that same summer. "Although the wagon wasn't always filled with furniture, the end result was always the same: the family needed money to survive the harsh conditions they were living under.

"Since then," she comments, "I've been convinced that poverty can be very destructive. Ingrained within me has been the thought that 'I'd better not let myself get that poor again.' I must admit that becoming poor is one of my greatest fears in this lifetime."

Bedroom Vision

Christopher is a thirty-six-year-old journalist, photographer, and former physician living in Connecticut. The younger of two brothers, he grew up Catholic in Newport Beach, California. "When I was a child," he recalls, "my life was idyllic. We lived on the beach, and I spent most of my time playing in the ocean or bicycling. My parents were warm and supportive. I prayed a lot, but felt that parochial school was unnecessary.

"One morning when I was about six, I awoke in my bed as usual and sat up for a minute or two. Suddenly I started to hear the most sublime and beautiful music coming from the left side of my room. I looked and saw an extraordinarily beautiful winged angel gliding through my room and playing a harp. My eyes were forced closed. I opened them again to see her form exit through the right wall.

"I felt happy but perplexed," comments Christopher. "It definitely wasn't a dream or a hypnagogic hallucination. I didn't tell my parents or anyone until about two months later.

"Then, while I was in catechism class, the nuns were talking about angels and celestial visitations. I cautiously raised my hand and related my bedroom experience. Very cuttingly, I was told, 'Angels only appear to saints and priests!' I felt quite embarrassed before the laughing reaction of my classmates.

"I never told anyone else about the experience, not even my parents. But I knew God was real because of it. Later in life I gained new insight, though.

"I've reflected that seeing the angel to my left and then to my right meant that I would be close to God early and late in life, and that my middle years would be muddled. This has indeed been true so far. The first part of my life was wonderful. Hopefully, the last part will be too."

The Cherubim

Eloise is a seventy-seven-year-old retired commercial artist and practical nurse who has spent most of her life in rural Iowa. An only child, she was raised in a Protestant home with little interest in mysticism. "Before the age of three," Eloise recalls, "whenever I felt like crying about something, almost at once I would experience the presence of two delightful beings. They had golden curly hair, blue eyes, and beautiful pink-and-white complexions. They wore loose-fitting dresses with a sash around the waist, and their feet were encased in something that resembled ballet slippers.

"The girls appeared to be about ten to twelve years of age, and their presence would always comfort me. Somehow I considered them as a link to paradise, though I knew that I couldn't go with them. They never spoke to me, but their sheer presence was joyful. As a result, I learned to pray to a Being that I could see only as a great white light that held comfort and love."

Eloise comments: "I know of no conversation, pictures, or experiences that could have triggered these events. Many decades later, I still know of no way to explain them. At present I read the Bible very slowly and reinterpret obscure passages. I consider myself a staunch Christian, though definitely not accepting any conventional church doctrines."

Awakening from Coma

Alison is a thirty-five-year-old woman living in southern California. She recalls: "At age seven, the tranquillity of my world was broken when my beloved grandfather was diagnosed as having lung cancer. Within a matter of weeks he became weaker than I'd ever seen him before. One day during this time grandpa asked me to clip his fingernails and comb his hair, because he didn't want 'the mortician to do these things.' We both had tears in our eyes and said our good-byes over the manicure.

"A few days later, grandpa lapsed into a coma that extended into weeks, and then into months. We kept him at home and cared for him. Abruptly one day grandpa awoke, totally coherent and seemingly strong.

"He said that his mother and father—and the Angel of Death too—were standing in the room waiting to take him, and he then begged them for more time. My uncle and aunt immediately called my mother, and she brought my baby brother beside him.

"My grandfather said goodbye to each of us in turn, all the while arguing with 'the Angel' to let him finish his message to each. At last he completed all his good-byes.

"Ten minutes after the last interview, grandpa slipped back into the coma. We kids were sent upstairs, and our family physician and the ambulance were immediately called. Though I was still in my room, I felt his soul pass as he died."

Alison comments: "My grandfather had been the most important loving force in my life, because my own parents had created a tension-ridden home environment. Yet the grieving process that had begun for me on the day of his diagnosis, nine months before, ended on that day. I only wish that grandpa could have lived longer as I grew older."

The Faraway Kingdom

Monica is a twenty-nine-year-old woman living in suburban Maryland. Raised in a strict Catholic home, she regularly attended a parochial day school for twelve years. "When I was about six to ten, I had a made-up world where I was a little girl from a faraway land who attended a boarding school. In this world, my father was a king where we came from: a magical king. He was very loving and infinitely kind and patient. He could 'poof' anything out of thin air, so that I never lacked for anything material. He could also 'poof' himself in and out of rooms.

"I can't remember if I was magical, too. I think I was, but not as magical as my father. The teachers in this imaginary boarding school were nuns who knew of our special abilities. Interestingly, I don't think I had a mother in my make-believe world.

"Sometimes, in real life," recalls Monica, "I would take metal staples at home and pull them apart. These became coins from our faraway land. This particular memory is significant to me, because it meant that having enough money was never a concern there—just as there was never a shortage of metal staples at home, so too was there never a shortage of money in my fantasy world."

Especially since the recent birth of her first child, Monica has given much thought to her youthful imagination. "There are some strange twists," she observes. "Why wouldn't I have included a mother—a basic bond to any child—in my world? It wasn't indicative of my own family situation, as my parents have been happily married through my entire life. Why would I have conjured a boarding school, instead of the conventional parochial school I was attending? Why did we come from far away? What could this boarding school offer me that I couldn't get back home? Why was my father a magical king? And why was I also magical, different from all the other students at school?"

After a great deal of thinking, Monica has arrived at satisfying answers. "They lie in my realization that my imaginary world, though simplistic and surrealist, is remarkably analogous to my spiritual development and to how I view reality and spirit. That is, I know that I'm a spark of God—magical, yes, but not as advanced. I now regard earthly life as resembling a boarding school—a classroom, a place to visit, in order to learn, grow, and become.

"Undoubtedly, I intuitively knew more as a child than my religious upbringing stressed. The truth was there, disguised, to be sure, but acted out in my make-believe world. Now that I'm a mother," Monica concludes, "the nurturing of childhood spirituality is especially important to me."

10
Unforgettable Dreams

*A dream that is not remembered might as well have not
been dreamt, and therefore a dream forgotten and gone
from mind is never fulfilled.*

—THE *ZOHAR* [BOOK OF SPLENDOR]

*D*REAMS have fascinated nearly every culture in
recorded history. The ancients regarded dreams with
respect and even awe, considering them to herald
important messages for daily life. During their golden age, the
Greeks built more than three hundred temples in homage to
the god of medicine, Asclepius. Seekers would travel long
distances to these temples and participate in sacred rituals
designed to elicit a healing dream. In the Orient, too, dream
incubation temples were similarly erected in serene and peaceful settings.

Native American tribes prized dreams as a wellspring of
inspiration. Their shamans would journey deep into the wilderness, where, fasting in isolation, they would induce a
dream of power or knowledge to provide guidance for their
people. Occasionally a youthful dream experienced during a
vision quest would have a lifetime impact on both the dreamer
and other tribal members.

In our own society we seem to have forgotten such intuitive

wisdom. From our earliest years we are taught either to ignore our dreams completely or to dismiss them as inherently trivial. Almost never are children encouraged to remember and relate their dreams. By adhering to this attitude as we reach adulthood, we inevitably fragment ourselves and lose touch with a valuable source of inspiration.

The narratives that follow are varied in their content and symbolism, imagery and underlying message. Yet they all represent childhood dreams that have proven memorable and of lasting importance to their dreamers. By heeding our own dreams more carefully, we may likewise find greater wholeness and direction for everyday living.

The Figure on the Hill

Joyce is a thirty-five-year-old woman living in rural Michigan. Her parents were not churchgoers, and she received little exposure to religious teaching. Nevertheless, at the age of four Joyce experienced an unusually intense spiritual dream:

"It's dusk on a summer's day, and the sun is large and red, setting to my left. I am walking in a northerly direction up a hill in the countryside. No one else is there. I am walking among tall pine trees as the wind rustles them.

"I come to a clearing near the top of the hill and begin to feel frightened by the growing darkness. To my right is a church. It's a simple, white building with approximately five stairs up to the entrance. No lights are on. To my left are more trees, and the sky is becoming even darker.

"Right in front of me I see a large, bright, white, transparent figure coming toward me, until he stands right next to me. He is no longer so transparent, and I see that he is beautiful, with light brown hair and brilliant blue eyes that look right through me. He wears a white, foot-length garment, like a robe, with a belt of gold and a light blue sash.

"The figure takes my hand and says, 'Don't be afraid. I'll always be with you.' "

Joyce remembers: "At that point, everything disappeared and I awoke feeling wonderfully happy and joyous. It was like no other dream I'd ever experienced. I was so excited and tried telling everyone what had happened. But no one paid any attention to me. Eventually I stopped relating it to people I knew and went about my everyday life.

"Decades passed, and when I was thirty, I became very ill. The dream came back to my memory in a very vivid way, and I comprehended aspects that weren't understandable when I was a child."

"The Human Diet"

Nicole is a sixteen-year-old high school student living in rural Minnesota. Her parents divorced when she was two, and she grew up with her mother and brother. The granddaughter of a Lutheran minister, Nicole attended Lutheran elementary school. "One night when I was about nine," she recalls, "I had an extremely vivid dream. It was like a still color photograph of a starving, dying African child. It wasn't like the pictures you see on commercials; it was too disturbing. The child—a boy— was the most emaciated possible without being dead. Below the photograph in bold letters was the caption THE HUMAN DIET.

"I couldn't put the dream out of my mind," Nicole continues, "and I thought about it often over the weeks and months that passed. Finally, when I became older, I interpreted the dream as a message about the wastefulness of meat eating and the relevance of vegetarianism.

"That is, if we change the human diet to one that's more in harmony with nature, then we could accomplish so much. We would help reduce the suffering of animals, alleviate human health problems caused by eating high-fat diets, reduce environmental waste, and end human starvation caused by the animal industry.

"Now that I'm planning to attend college soon," Nicole explains, "the dream is helping to define my purpose in the world: to study nutrition and try my best in aiding humanity."

The Missing Pin

Lucy is a seventy-one-year-old retired administrative assistant living in Los Angeles. An only child, she grew up in rural Pennsylvania in a Methodist family. At the age of eight Lucy and her stepfather visited her great aunt Margaret, living on the Lake Erie shore. Margaret's young daughter Mary had died some fifteen years before, and as a special gift, Margaret gave Lucy a lovely little lapel pin shaped like a pair of ballet slippers. It had been Mary's favorite "dress-up" pin, as she had wanted to be a ballerina.

"I treasured that pin," recalls Lucy, "and though I had never met her, somehow I felt close to the little girl who had died so young. The pin went everywhere with me. Perhaps two years passed, and one day I lost the pin.

"I cried and cried, and my mother and I looked everywhere for it. But we couldn't find the pin. I felt heartbroken and, about a week later, decided to 'talk' with Mary before I went to sleep. Speaking quietly beside my bed, I told Mary how sorry and sad I felt for losing her favorite treasure. That same night, I experienced a very vivid dream:

"I was sitting on the sofa in our living room doing my

homework as usual, when I saw the little pin float up, from behind the sofa, with tiny wings on its sides.

"When I awoke it was morning, and the dream was incredibly vivid. I ran into the living room and told my mother. Together we moved the sofa away from the wall, and there, nestled down in the carpet by the floorboard, was the treasured ballerina pin."

Lucy comments: "I instantly knew then—and I still fervently believe—that Mary put that dream into my thoughts, somehow. I still have the little pin, and though it's missing a stone or two, it's just as beautiful as when I received it sixty-two years ago."

Goddess of the Catacombs

Marcella is a thirty-two-year-old visual artist and licensed hypnotherapist living in Santa Cruz, California. Born and raised a Catholic in Germany, she has spent the last ten years within the United States. "My key childhood experience," Marcella recalls, "was a recurring dream when I was between six and twelve years of age:

"I am standing in a type of underground catacombs or temple, perhaps in some ancient time. I don't know at all how I got here. The structure is dimly lit, and I can see some of my surroundings. There are tall pillars that form arches, and the colors are earth tones of mauve and brown. The space around me is about the size of a large room, and I feel secure and safe.

"The major feature of this structure is a statue of the Virgin Mary. It appears to be in need of repair. Nevertheless, I intuitively sense that I have been brought to this place to see and honor this statue of her.

"I experienced this dream repetitively as a girl, but didn't really understand it at the time," Marcella recollects. "Initially, I shared it with my friends, but they starting teasing me about being 'so religious.' Finally, I stopped talking about it altogether.

"Today," Marcella comments, "I'm very active in spiritual matters and have been leading a women's spirituality group for two years. I understand my childhood dream as an early initiation in helping to restore the goddess—the feminine—to its rightful place in present society."

The Vanished Lover

Dawn is a thirty-nine-year-old staff member at a university in Indiana. The youngest of six children, she grew up in a religiously active Presbyterian family in Cincinnati. "I was ten," Dawn recalls, "when I experienced a vivid dream that has subsequently affected my entire life:

"The scene is our backyard, and it's a lovely spring day. The trees are green, the flowers are budding. The sky is blue and radiant. I am deeply in love with a very handsome, dark-haired man with a Latin accent of some kind, and he loves me. We are wonderfully happy—ecstatic—together. We stand on the roof of my garage, and everyone comes out of their houses into their backyards to gaze at us. 'Transported by love' is how we feel. With a joyful expression, my beloved gives me a ruby ring.

"Then the dream somehow shifts. A huge crowd is now milling in our backyard, and the two of us have become separated. I quickly look around, but can't find my beloved. Growing more anxious, I begin searching everywhere for him. Another man comes by, and he's very similar in appearance to my betrothed. But as I look at him carefully, I see that he's not the same, and sense that he's evil.

"Suddenly I think that I see my beloved's body lying amid a pile of newspapers at the base of a tree. I madly search through all the papers, but to no avail. He's still missing, and we're still separated from one another."

Dawn continues: "Then I woke up. And when I awoke, I was still surrounded and suffused by love. For the next three days I walked around dazed in that love. Throughout my childhood and adolescence, when my friends at age ten, eleven, or fifteen would say, 'I love so-and-so,' I would reply inside myself, 'No, that's not love. *I* know what love is.'

"That is, I felt that my strange, wonderful dream had come from God, because a ten-year-old girl couldn't know that kind of love unless God had shown her.

"I believe that this dream vividly taught me that the first principle of God is love. Growing into adulthood, I therefore regarded love as the most important thing in life. After my first marriage ended very painfully, I actually started to feel betrayed by the dream. But a wise old man advised me to use it as a compass.

"In this way I began to feel my way again in life, asking myself, 'Is this experience more like the love in the dream?' and steering myself *toward* those things, and 'Is this experience less like the love in the dream?' and steering myself *away* from those.

"I'm a practicing Quaker," Dawn observes, "and I still don't know why God showed this love to me in a childhood dream. Nevertheless, I firmly believe that everything is possible through God. I have a deep faith in Quaker decision making, which is based in worship—and the teaching that if we seek to be led by God, then God will lead us in the way we need to go."

Dream of the Crusades

Susan, the middle-aged Florida woman whom we met in chapter 4, relates: "As a child about four, I had a vivid and perhaps repetitive dream:

"I hold a baby in my arms, while someone authoritative tells me, 'If you say Jesus is the Christ, then you will be killed.' I clutch my baby to my breast and reply, 'I will not deny it.'

"The dream made a very strong impression on me, though I never understood its source," Susan comments. "I never forgot it. More than thirty years later, I attended college and took a course in world history and civilization. When the professor began lecturing about the Crusades, I felt convinced that my early dream had represented a past life in that era. It was eerie. Yet I had always sensed the reality of reincarnation, though it was certainly never taught in my hard-shell rural Baptist upbringing in the Ohio Valley."

Message from Grandfather

Jonathan, the professional singer whom we met in chapter 5, relates: "My grandfather died when I was eleven. To my knowledge, he was a righteous and extraordinary person. We had spent a lot of time together. He was humble, gentle, and wise. His face clearly radiated wisdom and warmth.

"I had done a lot of rebelling when I reached puberty, and yet I always felt deep down that my grandfather's eye was still upon me. Then, in high school, I started associating with a 'bad crowd' of boys, out of a rebellious attitude, I guess. It was a stupid thing to do, but at the time I wouldn't listen to my parents or older brothers.

"Then one night I went to bed and had a very vivid dream. My grandfather appeared and spoke to me. He gently but firmly asked many direct questions about my conduct. At first I started to reply defensively, but then I knew that he was right about every point. It was like no other dream I had ever experienced.

"When I awoke," Jonathan concludes, "the experience was still fresh as could be. I strongly felt that my grandfather had come to guide me. Right then I decided to break off my association with the 'bad crowd' of boys, and did so. In a way, the dream may have been a turning point in my life, for soon after, I began studying more seriously and changing my attitude about a lot of things."

Moving through Starry Space

Helen, the instructional technologist whom we met in chapters 5 and 9, recalls: "One night when I was about seven, I had a strange and vivid dream:

"There is a triangular cluster of spheres moving at tremendous speed through dark, star-speckled space. I know that the spheres are moving, yet as I look, they appear to be standing still. That the spheres are simultaneously in motion and yet standing still perplexes but doesn't disturb me. As I gaze at this strange scene, I feel deeply in touch with something vital and good. I feel highly energized, blissful, at peace, and in harmony.

"When I awoke," Helen remembers, "the dream was still very vivid, and I never forgot it. Years later, a science teacher explained that if I was moving at the same speed as the spheres, then they would appear to be standing still. This felt like an accurate explanation of what had occurred in the dream.

"I have remembered relatively few dreams in my entire life," observes Helen. "This was one of only two or three that were absolutely vivid—in fact, more clear than ordinary, waking consciousness." Today Helen traces her strong interest in spirituality to her youthful dream and a few other intense, early experiences. "They led me to a strong sense that we're ultimately in good hands. My childhood experiences make it virtually impossible to take the position that any one spiritual path is the *only* one."

Life's Hidden Side

Jean, the retired office worker whom we met in chapter 9, recounts: "I had a strong sense about God, but had many unanswered questions while growing up. One night when I was about thirteen, though, I had a dream that became a key lesson for me:

"I'm holding a beautiful piece of fine fabric in my hands. As I fully admire it, slowly it's turned over so that I can now see its underside, which is incredibly more beautiful than the visible portion.

"When I awoke, I had a very warm and secure feeling, and I never forgot this dream. I don't think I really discussed it much with others, though. It seemed too private. Eventually I came to understand that the top side of the fabric represented my life as it would seem externally, or most superficially. The underside of the fabric represented *God's hidden workings*.

"Decades later, this youthful dream continues to guide me," comments Jean. "I've come to believe that what appears to us as evil may in actuality be a temporary and slight digression from absolute reality or perfection, if we could only see the entire picture as God sees it. His providence is so utilitarian and, at the same time, so simple, it is awesome."

The Shining Plaza by the Sea

Sally is a thirty-six-year-old artist and mother living in Bozeman, Montana. As a preschooler she lived in a residential section of New York City. "There was a pretty oval park outside our apartment building," Sally recalls, "and several blocks away stood a large department store where my grandmother worked. In those idyllic days my mother and I often strolled over to visit her there. My grandmother loved me—and still does—in a way that comes as close as I can imagine to unconditional love. Sometime during those years I had a repetitive dream or vision:

"I walk out of our apartment building and toward my grandmother's store. I am alone. The oval park has vanished. Instead, I am walking out onto a vast plaza of mother of pearl shimmering gently in the sunlight. The plaza is semicircular, and I walk toward the far, curved edge. It is bounded by a low colonnade of white marble. I see that beyond it lies a boundless ocean, aquamarine and sparkling. The sky is clear, brightly and serenely blue. I am filled with infinite joy, expansiveness, and peace."

Sally remarks: "I've carried this image like a talisman all my life, wondering how to align with its powerful and beautiful message. Several years ago I used it as the basis for a visualization-relaxation exercise in a class I was teaching for expectant mothers. It proved very helpful for them.

"Lately I find my vision serving as a kind of 'background music' to my daily life and my relations with other people. When the vision is most clearly present in my mind's eye, I feel assured that I'm centered, and living and responding from my higher self."

Sally adds wistfully, though: "Sometimes I wonder: What would my life have been like had I begun to act sooner on my childhood vision?"

11

Understanding and Honoring Childhood Spirituality

I struggle, I yield and love, I become that child.
—CONRAD AIKEN

THE topic of childhood spirituality is finally gaining the long-awaited attention it richly deserves. For many different and important reasons today, psychology is recognizing that each of us is born with an innate spirituality that longs for expression and nourishment. It is becoming increasingly clear that reconnecting with our inner child is vital to the process of emotional healing, recovery, and general well-being. The mechanistic view of the human personality, which at one time was nearly unchallenged within the mainstream, is no longer credible. It has certainly become obsolete in most current therapeutic approaches. Still lacking, though, has been real, empirical information about the spiritual aspects of our earliest years.

Visions of Innocence has been written to help remedy this situation. In the preceding nine chapters, we have had the opportunity to hear from many individuals recounting key and uplifting experiences during childhood. Undoubtedly reflecting the diversity of periodicals and newspapers in which my initial author's query was published, the sample of respondents was quite broad. It included homemakers and clergy, secretaries and doctors, teachers and psychologists, nurses and business managers, actors and playwrights, artists and musicians.

The interviewees had grown up in many different places—some rural, such as in Montana, New Hampshire, West Virginia, Nova Scotia, or pastoral southern England. Others were raised in affluent suburban locales. Still others grew to adolescence in major cities like New York or Los Angeles. Most hailed from the United States, with smaller numbers from Canada and England, and a handful from Australia, the Caribbean, Germany, and Switzerland.

Although the majority of respondents were at least nominally from Catholic or various Protestant backgrounds, the extent of their youthful church involvement varied widely. As children, some had eagerly attended parochial school for many years and participated actively in church activities. Conversely, others had felt indifference or even antipathy toward their formal religious training, whatever its content. A significant minority of interviewees were raised in households that were either at least nominally Jewish or else wholly nonaffiliated.

Rather surprisingly, the respondents also ranged considerably in their chronological age. Mistakenly, I had expected that nearly all would be members of the baby-boom counterculture generation (or younger) who were intrigued by the topic through raising their own small children. Although most were in their thirties or forties, a sizable proportion were older, and more than a few were grandparents (or great-grandparents) in their seventies and eighties. Thus the interviewees were just as varied in chronological age as they were in their occupational, geographic, and religious backgrounds. In short, my sample was definitely broad-based, and hardly restricted to a particular subgroup within American society.

Many of the narratives have been dramatic or poetic. Some even resemble synopses for alluring short stories or film productions. Yet they have scarcely been elicited from around the globe, carefully analyzed, and then systematically organized for this book merely to offer entertainment; they have a real theoretical contribution to make. What significant conclusions, then, can we draw from them? How can we best place these highly diverse reports into a meaningful and orderly pattern?

Understanding Childhood Spirituality

Most fundamentally, it now appears undeniable that some of us (perhaps far more than we suspect) have undergone tremendous peak—even mystical—experiences during our early years. In this respect, conventional psychology and its allied disciplines have painted a badly incomplete portrait of childhood and, by extrapolation, of adulthood as well. For no approach that ignores our highest proclivities can possibly claim to be either fully valid or comprehensive. As a growing number of influential therapists and educators are far more accurately depicting, we all have an inborn capacity for deeply spiritual encounters with the world around us; Abraham Maslow's intuitive hunch in this respect has been posthumously proven correct.

Of course, lacking the appropriate vocabulary and concepts, most youngsters are unable to articulate these episodes.

Nearing their teens, some may succeed in conveying impassioned though fragmentary descriptions; small children rarely can communicate even that much. But that hardly renders their experiences meaningless or illegitimate. Indeed, from the recollections of varied respondents now in their elderly years, numinous moments of childhood can exert a profound and lifetime impact.

Secondly, these reports indicate that a variety of different types of exalted experience are possible during childhood. Confirming the results of earlier investigators, I have found that near-death encounters (NDEs) can be powerful and transformative, even for very young children. These can induce a lifelong interest in mystical teachings and impart a sense of abiding security about the human soul and its continuity in a higher world.

Yet, also validating the speculation of prominent NDE researchers like Kenneth Ring, it is now apparent that we need not undergo a close brush with death to acquire such an outlook. Clearly, one key trigger of youthful ecstasy is exposure to the natural world's splendor, such as majestic mountains, wild forests, and vast ocean vistas. This finding substantiates the viewpoint of Romantic poets like Wordsworth, who contended nearly two hundred years ago that childhood is a time of particular sensitivity to nature's grandeur. Many of the narratives presented here, moreover, indicate that ineffable experiences can be evoked by far more ordinary natural surroundings. The childhood doorway to transcendence may lie hidden within a flowering garden, a grove of trees, the scampering play of squirrels, or even a pebbled plot of grass with insects.

Most reports, however, were wholly independent of nature. For some people, the trigger was an act of heartfelt, spontaneous prayer or a more formalized religious moment that catapulted them into a timeless and transcendent state. For others, deep contemplation about self-identity, or life and death, had a powerfully uplifting effect. Strikingly, there is almost no research within mainstream psychology to suggest that children may become absorbed—let alone uplifted—by such key philosophical or metaphysical questions.

For still others, the catalyst for spiritual awakening involved a visionary episode, a dream experience, or simply an ordinary moment of daily life that suddenly became an entry point to bliss. Clearly, there are many different pathways by which children may reach an exalted awareness. At the very least, we need to be more sensitive to this fact in child-rearing and educational practice.

Another intriguing finding is that aesthetics can be a gateway for childhood spirituality. We are certainly familiar with tales of remarkably precocious composers like Mozart and Beethoven. Obviously, to write a sonata at the age of four requires an awesome natural talent. But in a different sense, it may be that many of us, as children, are far more stirred by music and art than is generally recognized. Public schools in the United States and elsewhere have generally regarded such activities as mere frills. Yet as far back as the turn of the twentieth century, iconoclastic educators like Rudolf Steiner (founder of the international network of Waldorf schools) strongly argued for the centrality of aesthetics in all facets of education. With the recent emergence of art and music therapy as legitimate professional fields, perhaps this situation will begin to change for the better.

As we have seen, the vast majority of reports in this book have described supernal experiences that occurred well outside the halls of church or synagogue. In several cases, the child had received virtually no formal religious exposure whatsoever. We therefore cannot say that sectarian worship or study is essential for children to gain a sense of the numinous. The evidence simply does not show this. Yet for some children, participating in formal religious services or reading sacred books like the Bible were very real openings to unitive experience. In addition, many people regarded their youthful transcendent episodes as definitely related to their early religious training, or more meaningful because of it.

Is there a way of resolving this perplexing issue? Perhaps the problem lies not with organized religion itself, but rather in how it is presented to youngsters inhabiting a society radically different from what existed just a few generations ago. In other words, the methods that were effective for clergy and religious educators in the past may no longer be successful. The solution seems to be that formal religion—at least for children, if not most adults as well—must be reenergized to become salient: to become a helpmeet, not a hindrance.

This matter leads to a final, and intimately related, issue. Over and over again, individuals in this study reported that they had no one with whom to share their intense spiritual experience. Sometimes they tried to communicate with parents, siblings, peers, or clergy, only to give up after receiving polite indifference. Others fared worse, encountering disparagement, ridicule, or even insulting doubts about their emotional health. As a result, some had to wait long years into adulthood before discovering through books or teachers that such beatific episodes have been basic to human experience for millennia.

In this respect, religious educators can help children immeasurably by validating and honoring these wondrous moments so rarely acknowledged in our contemporary world. This does not mean that every unusual account offered by youngsters should be accepted at face value. But it is meant to emphasize that by paying greater attention to children's spiritual experiences, we can exert a beneficial influence that can last a lifetime. Specifically, then, what can we do to better foster this natural quality in children today?

Implications for Parents and Educators

Certainly, children inwardly differ widely from one another, just as do adults. Yet the wide-ranging reports we have heard clearly support the notion that every child is born with an innate spiritual essence that parents and relatives, educators and clergy—indeed, all who are involved with youngsters—can do much to enhance. We need not be saints or mystical adepts to be successful at this task. The important thing is to begin, to make the effort. Especially because we live in a society whose mass media and public institutions generally denigrate our higher qualities, it is crucial that we become active in this domain. I am convinced that a laissez-faire approach (however well intentioned) nowadays will offer children little help in safeguarding their inborn spiritual sensitivity.

Rooted in actual experience rather than vague or abstract speculation about childhood's peak moments, the narratives in this book offer us valuable direction. Consequently, here are five general principles—by no means intended as all-inclusive—for nurturing your child's spirituality in everyday life.

THE GATEWAY OF NATURE

Actively expose your child to nature. As visionary poets like Blake and Wordsworth have long been aware, closeness to nature during our early years can have a profound effect on our spiritual development. If you live in a city, take your child on frequent trips into the countryside throughout the seasons to better experience the subtle rhythms of life. Visits to special wilderness places like the desert or the mountains can be particularly potent. Uplifting experiences may occur that will last a lifetime.

Strengthen your child's daily bond with nature by encouraging care for pets or plants. Become involved in helping to raise a garden or even a windowsill flowerbox. These are wonderful ways for children to stay balanced and gentle.

THE IMAGINATIVE JOURNEY

Always seek to affirm your child's imagination and sense of wonder. Mystical teachers have long insisted that imagination is a vital tool for inner development. Yet most contemporary schools and other societal institutions dampen this natural, vibrant quality in children. Recognize that by praising your child's fantasy and imaginative play, you are doing something quite important.

In fact, mere encouragement is not enough. Rather, actively join in the activity. Reading bedtime stories—or creating your own together with your child—is an excellent way to foster imagination. To help stimulate your child's sense of wonder, show your admiration for the splendor of seemingly ordinary events like sunsets, moonlit skies, and rainbows.

RITUALS

Whether you embrace a formal religion affiliated with a church or synagogue or a completely personal creed, maintain regular rituals in your home. When involving your child, these rituals can be as simple as lighting candles or blessing the food at your dinner table. The crucial thing is that they be meaningful expressions of your own spirituality and give you a heightened awareness of the transcendent that surrounds all things.

By definition, rituals involve physical activity or movement. They should be performed slowly and deliberately, with maximum awareness of the here-and-now. It is also desirable to schedule home rituals for specific moments of the day or week, as children generally need external structure more than adults. Oftentimes, you may wish to help your child create a ritual celebrating a birthday, graduation, or other special family event. Incorporating art and music (with recordings or live instruments) into such rituals will help make them a more memorable, multisensory experience. Here, too, let your child be as inventive as possible.

DREAMS: THE OPEN ROAD

Encourage your child to share dreams with you. Many ancient systems of knowledge have taught that dreams are a key means to self-realization. But they are typically ignored or even demeaned ("It was only a dream") in today's society.

If you show a genuine interest in your child's dreams, he or she will learn to value them and heed their messages for direction throughout later life. In this regard, your day-to-day encouragement is more important than your specific guidance in interpretation. Allow adequate time each morning for your child's recollection and your subsequent discussion.

Some children greatly enjoy drawing a picture of their dream or even acting it out with imaginative props. When you and your child share your dreams each morning after awakening, you are certainly strengthening your closeness and getting to know each other in a deeper way.

Of course, you need to use care in relating your dreams meaningfully to your child. Advice from a friend beforehand might be helpful in this regard. As a general policy, you might wish to select one of your dreams each week to share. Then record it alongside your child's in an illustrated "dream notebook" that you develop together. As your child grows, it will be fascinating for you to reread his or her dreams from earlier years.

THE GENTLE ART OF LISTENING

As a final principle here, always listen to your child as fully as possible. Remember: even the most exalted childhood experience may be very difficult to put into words. Yet it is precisely these moments, reflecting our spiritual essence, that make each of us truly unique. As many traditions emphasize, we are here on earth to develop our own particular talents and sensitivities.

Certainly, in our fast-paced and technological way of life, it is not always easy to find quiet moments. We all get tired or irritable with loved ones from time to time. But safeguarding your child's natural spirituality requires putting aside time each day to hear his or her joys, triumphs, and frustrations. Avoid artificial, "Let's sit and talk now" situations. Instead, call it "art time," and let each of you draw pictures or engage in crafts while sitting at the same table. Or simply go for a long walk together, away from intrusive distractions.

Be assured that such moments honor the special relationship you have with your child and, ultimately, honor the divine spark that lies within all of us.

Guidelines for Future Exploration

Although this research about childhood spirituality has offered a variety of intriguing findings, they are by no means intended as definitive. Limitations in the makeup of the sample group raise several issues that can be resolved only through further empirical work. Perhaps most strikingly, more than two-thirds of the respondents to my author's query were women. Since American men are generally recognized to be uncomfortable about gazing inward, this result was not surprising. Nevertheless, it immediately raises the question: Are girls more likely to undergo intensely spiritual experiences than boys? If so, is this difference due primarily to the influence of biology, upbringing, or a combination of the two? Or, conversely, are boys just as apt to have such uplifting episodes, but more prone to suppress them afterward?

My own hunch leans toward the latter hypothesis, for a simple reason. Major gender differences in how we communicate with one another indicate that by elementary school age, girls spend far more time sharing feelings than do boys. If so, then the old adage "Out of sight, out of mind" may well explain the relative paucity of numinous childhood memories for men: things we don't talk about, we tend to forget.

Of course, the big difference in response rate between the sexes in my study has another possible cause: that men are simply less interested in being interviewed about their early experiences—perhaps because of internalized pressures about time or privacy. Only additional exploration will tell. It will also be interesting to discover if boys are more prone to certain *types* of intense spiritual encounters than are girls. As yet, our number of cases is too small to form definite conclusions. It does appear, though, that boys are most likely to undergo "simple moments of ecstasy" or "profound musings." In contrast, girls are most apt to experience "backyard visions," "uncanny perceptions," or "unforgettable dreams."

Certainly, considerably more information is needed on cross-cultural differences with regard to inspirational moments of childhood. For instance, very few of my cases represent African American, Asian, Caribbean, Hispanic, or Native American backgrounds. Nor were there significant numbers involving upbringing in non-Western religions like Buddhism, Hinduism, or Islam. In follow-up work, it will undoubtedly be fascinating to compare the accounts of such individuals with those interviewed in this study.

Finally, it will also be important to learn whether numinous or blissful episodes during our early years are related to specific patterns of family life. For example, several respondents explicitly commented that their victimization through abuse or incest somehow led them to find uplifting inner resources that might not have emerged in more pleasant circumstances. Does a parallel therefore exist to near-death experiences and their transformative power? More evidence is definitely needed on this and many other matters pertaining to youthful spirituality.

As we enter a new global era, there is particular urgency in finding those aspects of human experience that transcend the ethnic and nationalistic differences that can divide us. By understanding and honoring our highest childhood qualities, we can help create a more peaceful and harmonious world.

Notes

1. Matthew Fox, *The Coming of the Cosmic Christ* (San Francisco: Harper, 1988), p. 181.
2. Tom Brown, *The Vision* (New York: Berkley Publishing Group, 1988), pp. 14–15.
3. John (Fire) Lame Deer and Richard Erdoes, *Lame Deer, Seeker of Visions* (New York: Simon and Schuster, 1972).
4. William Wordsworth, cited in Hunter Davies, *William Wordsworth: A Biography* (New York: Atheneum, 1980), p. 24.
5. Professor B. Knight, cited in A. Charles Babenroth, *English Childhood: Wordsworth's Treatment of Childhood in the Light of English Poetry* (New York: Columbia University Press, 1922), p. 374.
6. Ibid., p. 375.
7. C. G. Jung, *Memories, Dreams, Reflections* (New York: Vintage Books, 1965), pp. 14–15.
8. Ibid., p. 20.
9. Elisabeth Kübler-Ross, *On Children and Death* (New York: Collier, 1985), p. 206.
10. Ibid., p. 219.
11. John L. Bradshaw, *Healing the Shame That Binds You* (Deerfield Beach, Fla.: Health Communications, 1988).
12. Portions of this narrative appeared in Dov. B. Edelstein, *Worlds Torn Asunder* (New York: Ktav, 1985), pp. 36–37.

Epigraph Sources

Chap. 1: C. G. Jung, "The Psychology of the Child Archetype," in *The Archetypes and the Collective Unconscious*, Vol. 9/1 of *The Collected Works of C. G. Jung*, translated by R. F. C. Hull (Princeton, N.J.: Princeton University Press, 1977), p. 162.

Chap. 2: Henry David Thoreau, *In Wildness Is the Preservation of the World*, selections and photos by Eliot Porter (San Francisco: Sierra Club Books, 1967), p. 19.

Chap. 3: Abraham H. Maslow, *Religions, Values, and Peak Experiences* (New York: Viking Press, 1972), p. x.

Chap. 4: *The Illustrated Jerusalem Bible*, edited by M. Friedlander (Jerusalem: Jerusalem Bible Company), p. 1423.

Chap. 5: Black Elk, cited in *A Treasury of Traditional Wisdom* by Perry Whitehall (New York: Simon and Schuster, 1971), p. 522.

Chap. 6: Conrad Aiken, "A Letter from Li Po," in *Selected Poems* (New York: Oxford University Press, 1969), p. 248.

Chap. 7: James Agee and Walker Evans, *Let Us Now Praise Famous Men* (New York: Ballantine, 1974), p. 54.

Chap. 8: William Blake, *The Complete Writings*, edited by Geoffrey Keynes (New York: Oxford University Press, 1966).

Chap. 9: *The Oxford Annotated Bible,* edited by Herbert G. May and Bruce M. Metzger (New York: Oxford University Press, 1962), p. 864.

Chap. 10: *Zohar*, translated by Harry Sperling and Maurice Simon (London: Soncino Press, 1934), vol. 2, p. 258.

Chap. 11: Aiken, "No, I Shall Not Say," in *Selected Poems*, p. 11.

Bibliogr

Agee, James, and Evans, Walker.   Men.
New York: Ballantine, 1974.

Aiken, Conrad. *Selected Poem*   ersity
Press, 1969.

Andersen, Hans Christian. *It'*   *Stories.*
Translated by Paul Leyssac   *,* 1938.

Babenroth, A. Charles. *Engl..*   *s Treat-*
ment of Childhood in the Light of Engns.   w York:
Columbia University Press, 1922.

Blake, William. *The Complete Writings.* Edited by Geoffrey Keynes.
New York: Oxford University Press, 1966.

Blofeld, John. *Beyond the Gods.* New York: Dutton, 1974.

Bradshaw, John L. *Healing the Shame That Binds You.* Deerfield
Beach, Fla.: Health Communications, 1988.

_____. *Homecoming: Reclaiming and Championing Your Inner
Child.* New York: Bantam, 1992.

Brown, Tom. *The Vision.* New York: Berkley Publishing Group,
1988.

Cheney, Sheldon. *Men Who Have Walked with God.* New York:
Alfred A. Knopf, 1966.

Coles, Robert. *The Moral Life of Children.* Boston: Atlantic
Monthly Press, 1986.

_____. *The Spiritual Life of Children.* Boston: Houghton Mifflin,
1990.

Elkind, David. *The Hurried Child.* Reading, Mass.: Addison-
Wesley, 1981.

Fox, Matthew. *The Coming of the Cosmic Christ*. San Francisco: Harper, 1988.

Greeley, Andrew M. *The Mary Myth: On the Femininity of God*. New York: Seabury Press, 1977.

Heller, David. *Talking to Your Child about God*. New York: Bantam, 1988.

Hoffman, Edward. *The Right to be Human: A Biography of Abraham Maslow*. Los Angeles: Jeremy P. Tarcher, 1988.

————. *The Way of Splendor: Jewish Mysticism and Modern Psychology*. Northvale, N.J.: Jason Aronson, 1989.

Hunter, Davies. *William Wordsworth: A Biography*. New York: Atheneum, 1980.

James, William. *The Varieties of Religious Experience*. Garden City, N.Y.: Doubleday, 1978.

Johnston, Francis. *Fatima: The Great Sign*. Rockford, Ill.: Tan Books, 1980.

Jung, C. G. *The Archetypes and the Collective Unconscious*. Vol. 9/1 of *The Collected Works of C.G. Jung*. Translated by R.F.C. Hull. Princeton, N.J.: Princeton University Press, 1980.

————. *Memories, Dreams, Reflections*. Recorded and edited by Aniela Jaffé. Translated by Richard and Clara Winston. New York: Vintage Books, 1965.

Kritsberg, Wayne. *Adult Children of Alcoholics Syndrome: From Discovery to Recovery*. Deerfield Beach, Fla.: Health Communications, 1986.

Kübler-Ross, Elisabeth. *On Children and Death*. New York: Collier, 1985.

Lame Deer, John (Fire), and Erdoes, Richard. *Lame Deer: Seeker of Visions*. New York: Simon and Schuster, 1972.

Lindsay, Jack. *William Blake: His Life and Work*. London: Constable, 1978.

Mahdi, Louise Carus; Foster, Steven; and Little, Meredith. *Betwixt and Between: Patterns of Masculine and Feminine Initiation*. LaSalle, Ill.: Open Court Publishing Co., 1987.

Maslow, Abraham H. *Religions, Values, and Peak Experiences.* New York: Viking Press, 1970.

————. *Toward a Psychology of Being.* New York: Van Nostrand Reinhold, 1968.

Meigs, Cornelia; Eaton, Anne; Nesbitt, Elizabeth; and Viguers, Ruth Hill. *A Critical History of Children's Literature.* New York: Macmillan, 1953.

Miller, Alice. *Banished Knowledge: Facing Childhood Injuries.* Translated by Leila Vennewitz. New York: Doubleday, 1990.

————. *Thou Shalt Not Be Aware: Society's Betrayal of the Child.* Translated by Hildegard and Hunter Hannuman. New York: Penguin, 1990.

Moody, Raymond. *Life after Life.* New York: Bantam, 1977.

————. *The Light Beyond.* New York: Bantam, 1988.

————. *Reflections on Life after Life.* New York: Bantam, 1977.

Morse, Melvin. *Closer to the Light: Learning from the Near-Death Experiences of Children.* New York: Ballantine, 1990.

Neihardt, John G. *Black Elk Speaks.* Lincoln, Nebr.: University of Nebraska Press, 1961.

The Oxford Annotated Bible. Edited by Herbert G. May and Bruce M. Metzger. New York: Oxford University Press, 1962.

Postman, Neil. *The Disappearance of Childhood.* New York: Delacorte Press, 1982.

Ring, Kenneth. *Heading toward Omega: In Search of the Meaning of the Near-Death Experience.* New York: William Morrow, 1984.

————. *Life at Death: A Scientific Investigation of the Near-Death Experience.* New York: Coward, McCann, and Geoghegan, 1980.

Sabom, Michael. *Recollections of Death: A Medical Investigation.* New York: Harper and Row, 1982.

Thoreau, Henry David. *In Wildness Is the Preservation of the World.* Selections and photos by Eliot Porter. San Francisco: Sierra Club Books, 1967.

Tolkien, J. R. R. *The Letters of J. R. R. Tolkien.* Selected and edited by Humphrey Carpenter. Boston: Houghton Mifflin, 1981.

Underhill, Evelyn. *Mysticism*. London: Methuen and Co., 1962.

Whitehall, Perry. *A Treasury of Traditional Wisdom*. New York: Simon and Schuster, 1971.

Whitfield, Charles L. *A Gift to Myself*. Deerfield Beach, Fla.: Health Communications, 1989.

————. *Healing the Child Within*. Deerfield Beach, Fla.: Health Communications, 1989.

William Wordsworth. Edited by Stephen Gill. New York: Oxford University Press, 1988.